BIG BOYS DON'T CRY

BIG BOYS DON'T CRY

Nick Battle

Authentic

MILTON KEYNES ● COLORADO SPRINGS ● HYDERABAD

14 13 12 11 10 09 08   8 7 6 5 4 3 2
Reprinted 2008

First published 2007 by Authentic Media
9 Holdom Avenue, Bletchley, Milton Keynes, Bucks, MK1 1QR, UK
1820 Jet Stream Drive, Colorado Springs, CO 80921, USA
OM Authentic Media, Medchal Road, Jeedimetla Village,
Secunderabad 500 055, A.P., India
www.authenticmedia.co.uk
Authentic Media is a division of IBS-STL U.K., limited by guarantee, with
its Registered Office at Kingstown Broadway, Carlisle, Cumbria CA3 0HA.
Registered in England & Wales No. 1216232. Registered charity 270162

British Library Cataloguing in Publication Data
A catalogue record for this book is available from the British Library.
978-1-86024-612-8

All photos are from the authors private collection except where stated.

Cover design by fourninezero design.
Cover photo black and white: Charlotte Banks
Cover photo colour: Tony Swain
Print management by Adare Carwin
Printed and bound in Great Britain by J.H. Haynes & Co., Sparkford

For Nicky

'Let There Be Love'

CONTENTS

ACKNOWLEDGEMENTS

Where to begin?

I guess with J.John and Gareth Brocklebank, who between them introduced me to Authentic Media and my publisher Malcolm Down. Thank you both.

To Alan Smith, former editor of the *New Musical Express*, mentor and friend.

Thank you for your encouragement.

To my dad and also to Ann Morrison for helping me to proofread and giving me invaluable feedback.

To Jonathan Cooke, and After the Fire for taking me on board thirty years ago, to the members of Fish Co. and Writz, thanks for living with the bass-playing basket case. I do hope what you find hidden in these pages won't be too shocking.

To all those it has been my great pleasure to work with over the years, and to my friends for doing the life miles with me.

The Edwards family, I would like to thank you for everything you have brought into my life, especially Lynn.

There are a few people without whom I would never have made it this far, so please, take a bow, Ryan and Verlon Battle, Willie Williams, Richard and Fran Morrison, Adrian and Judy Reith, Alan and Bev Sage-Smith, Trevor Von Trilsbach, Annie McCaig, Sue Ferguson-Lacey, Claire Goodman, Ian and Annette Slade, Mark and Alie Stibbe, David and Carrie Grant, J.John and Killy, Martyn and Joy Barter, Tony Swain, Alan and Sara Richards, Alan and Dawn Stokes, Mick Cater, Wyatt Ramsdale, Liz Ramsdale, Simon and Hilary Mayo, Tim's Trousers, Chris Briggs, Gordon Charlton, Hugh Goldsmith, Marc Fox and The Old Unrecoupables, Florence Macaulay,

Phylidda Vanstone, Iqbal and Kathie, Barry and Mary Kissell, Shirley and Arthur Hartup, Kipper and Lia Eldridge, Nick Corden, Gill Worthington, Margaret Knight, the Trevor family, David and Stephanie Blincow, John and Cynthia Dowding, Norman and Debbie Trotter, Michael and Jane Hastings, the mums of Christchurch school and the members of St Andrew's, Chorleywood this past fourteen years, and anybody else I may have forgotten, who at some point along the way has shown kindness to me, and I know there have been many.

To Malcolm Down: thank you for your faith in what is written and for your boldness in commissioning a book about my life. Thanks also for introducing me to Clive Price who has played a vital part in shaping the manuscript. It has been a very great privilege and pleasure to work with you both.

To Dad: what a journey! You are a great dad and I am proud to be your son. Thank you for everything.

To my daughters Misha and Jodie: you won't be proud of all you read in here, and I am sorry for that, as I am for the mistakes I've made. It has been my life, real and at times visceral; it has also been mostly fun. I pray that God would grant you both long, happy and fulfilling lives and that when trouble comes knocking that you would go to him first for help.

Misha: I know you love painting with words as much as I do; follow your creative dream.

Jodie: your sense of humour is fantastic, as is your ability to gather people around you. Enjoy life's dance.

To my wife, Nicky: I love you. Thank you for wanting to spend the rest of your life with me. You have brought me such great joy and happiness at a time when I'd just about given up on both. I am always yours.

Finally to my Lord and Saviour, Jesus. Thank you for restoring my soul.

'They that wait on the Lord shall renew their strength, run and not grow weary, walk and not faint.'

To God be the glory.

AND SO THIS IS CHRISTMAS

It was the wee small hours of Christmas Day when the ambulance men finally left. My mum had thrown up the last of her lethal cocktail. She had quaffed a deadly blend of Valium, Librium, Mogadon and whisky in a bid to make a final exit. My nana – seventy-two and blind – was lost in the horror of it all. I was kneeling on the floor of her two-up, two-down terraced house in Denton, Lancashire, staring at a picture of Jesus Christ (the one where the eyes stare back at you), pleading, 'Please God, please God – don't let my mum die. Please! Please!'

I was sixteen years old.

I prayed through the night. I knew, because Mum had stayed at home, it couldn't be that serious; yet I was still fearful. At six o'clock in the morning, I made a decision. I packed my rucksack and left the house. I started the long, slow walk through Hyde, towards Sheffield and my father's house. Along the way I hitched a lift over the Woodhead Pass to Barnsley.

On the way, the driver stopped to show me the grave from the Silkstone Mining Disaster of 1838, when twenty-six children were drowned by floodwater while working down Huskar Colliery. 'Take heed, watch and pray, for ye know not when the time is,' said the solemn inscription on the monument (which is still there to this day).

'Now, if there's a God in heaven, why did that happen?' said the driver.

I was spooked – and therefore much relieved – when he left me by the turn-off at the M1 near Barnsley. From there, I hitched a second lift to Tinsley by the steelworks, and finally took a cab to my dad's, in Riverdale Road, Sheffield.

It would be ten years before I would tell him what really happened that night, and why I turned up on his doorstep that morning.

It was a momentous year, 1957. Harold 'You've never had it so good' Macmillan became Prime Minister, triggering a boom-time for Britain. Lennon and McCartney met for the very first time, sparking a revolution in popular culture. The frisbee was invented, beginning a new craze on beaches and in parks across the world . . . oh yes, and I made my first appearance as well.

I was two weeks late. Initially, Mum had gone to Totnes Hospital for my birth. However, it would appear that she didn't want to push, and I didn't want to come out. So she was transferred to Torquay, where the midwife who finally delivered me had to have her arm in a sling for weeks as a result. Apparently, the left side of my face was all mashed up from the forceps. It seems I'd been a bit difficult.

Mum, who was extremely myopic anyway, haemorrhaged in her eyes, due to the strain of the birth. Her sight never really recovered – something she would remind me of from time to time as I grew up. Serving in the Royal Navy, Dad had also ended up at Torquay Hospital, with jaundice; something for which Mum never really forgave him. So he was not present when I was delivered.

By all accounts, Dad was a bit of a wild card back then, but seemed pretty popular with his mates; still, it wasn't long before he agreed to Mum's demands for him to leave the Royal Navy, and we moved to London. During the day Dad worked in a bank; he served in a restaurant at weekends, and also managed to work two evenings a week as a bouncer.

Times were tough and Mum was lonely. We were living in Teddington, and she missed my dad. She also missed her mum and sister Phyllis, who lived in her home town of Manchester. I'm told Mum started to drink a bit then. Not long after, my dad agreed to move back to Manchester, and we headed north to live near Nana and Aunty Phyllis. My dad worked for Roneo, and then NCR, selling accounting systems.

One of my earliest memories is of nursery school in Chorlton-Cum-Hardy in Manchester. It was the early sixties and the Russian cosmonaut Yuri Gagarin had just been the first man to orbit the earth in a spacecraft. For some strange reason, he came, of all places, to Manchester. We children stood at the school gates to cheer him on as his motorcade went by. From that moment on I wanted to be an astronaut. Later on, I wanted to be a vicar. Then, finally, at the grand old age of thirteen, I settled on being a musician. But that's jumping ahead a bit.

In the winter of 1963, we moved across the Pennines from Crumpsall in Manchester to Sheffield, and bought a semi-detached house in Hallamshire Road, Fulwood, for the princely sum of £3,000. Mum named our dwelling 'Witsend' apparently after Dad and me, who she claimed drove her to that point. I had my own bedroom with yellow Yogi Bear curtains, and a bright red carpet on the floor. The kitchen was made by Hygena, and we had teak G-Plan furniture, which was considered very cool at the time. When Dad was home, we used to play table tennis using the dining room table.

Around this time, my parents made friends with a couple called the Hilliers. They became a permanent fixture in our lives. They seemed to always be partying and playing mah-jong. There would be lots of booze, usually spirits; and, of course, everybody smoked. (After all, it was meant to be glam-orous, wasn't it?) I remember Dad putting me to bed some-times while these get-togethers would happen. He would stroke my forehead and say, 'Little man, you've had a busy day.' It made me feel soothed and safe.

Mum also became Akela of the local cub pack, 142nd Fulwood, Sheffield. It was a position she held for the best part of twenty years. She was awarded the Chief Scouts Medal of Merit, something I am proud to keep. Mum was an amazing lady; she had an appreciation of music and the arts, and a faith of sorts – kind of viewed through a glass darkly. She was shy, and yet could be the life and soul of the party; a romantic, yet at times she could be very cynical and sarcastic. She was a manipulator, yet fragile, a Christian and yet an alcoholic. She was vulnerable, sad, and yet possessed of a barbed sense of humour that she would consciously, or otherwise, sometimes turn and use on me.

Through a process of gradual osmosis, she instilled in me a sense of fear. And yet, she was my mum and I loved her.

Zany and creative, Mum painted using oils – I still treasure the oil painting of an American Indian she completed – and loved sculpting things out of clay. She used to make me little clay characters like a Paisley elephant and a dormouse tucked up in bed which she named Nicholas Mouse.

All of these things I keep. They remind me that despite Mum's problems and the deterioration later in life, once upon a time, I was loved by her.

2

THE TIES THAT BIND

My education in Sheffield commenced at Christchurch Infant School, Fulwood. I can remember accidentally on purpose tripping up one of my schoolmates who then sported a black eye. There wasn't any real malice in it – more a kind of curiosity as to what would happen. I didn't own up at the time, though.

Christchurch was also where I went to church. The deal was that the children stayed in for the first twenty minutes or so and then went to junior church, which I found very dull. I frequently used to duck out and play football with my mates.

Church was Anglican with a capital 'A'. But it wasn't bells and smells – more like pink hat with matching handbag and poodle. People considered themselves Christians and I guess they were, but the worship wasn't very eventful. The choir wore pale blue cassocks; there was one lady with a shrill alto voice whose tone, face – and 'Dame Edna' spectacles – will remain with me forever. The only light at the end of the tunnel was *Youth Praise*. This was a book of short, punchy hymns written in a supposedly 'pop' style. It's overwhelmingly cheesy now, but back then it was a break amid the boredom.

After leaving Christchurch, I went to Nether Green Junior School. I remember in my first year looking out of the window of the prefabricated hut as the hands of the clock swept to half-past three, and seeing Mum standing there, resplendent in her bright red coat, waiting for me.

I was bullied. And it wasn't until I learned the power of words and developed a sense of humour that I finally sussed how to survive. I wasn't particularly tall as a child, and quite often would get picked on. There used to be a river running at the bottom of our playground, and to reach it, we used to climb over a wall and down a ladder. On one occasion I'd nipped over the wall only to find that two boys had then pulled the ladder back up and left me. It was home time, and I can remember the blind panic welling up in me as to how I was ever going to escape and get home safely to Mum. After twenty minutes or so, the boys returned the ladder, noisily laughing at their mischievous deed. But to a little kid like me, it was very frightening.

Of course, some of the teachers stuck in my brain; one who had a strong Victorian streak of justice, another who looked like one of Mary Quant's models, had a beehive hairdo, the longest fingernails you had ever seen and a mini-skirt to die for – she was impossibly glamorous to my young eyes. I was smitten until the day she poked me with her false nails and broke the spell. How could there be a future for us, when she chastised me for trying to eat a vanilla ice cream with a knife and fork? Then there was the man who slippered all the boys in the class if he decided the standard of work wasn't good enough – thinking about that now, I bridle with the injustice of it all. There was also a teacher who took me aside one day and told me I had hands shaped like a musician. Perhaps she had the gift of prophecy – who knows!

Like many children, I was lucky enough to have a great nana, and from an early age I used to listen to her stories about the war. One of my nana's favourites concerned a bombing raid in Manchester. She was in the Civil Defence when she came across a naked man in the street. He was running down the road, with a piece of sharp glass sticking out of his bottom.

'Nana,' I asked, 'what was he saying?'

'Ooh me arse, me bleedin' arse!' she replied, without a trace of irony.

She had snow-white hair, was diminutive in stature, but a powerhouse and a survivor. I remember her having beautiful, kind, hazel eyes and a warm Lancashire accent – coupled with bag-loads of charm and charisma. She used to travel over regularly from Manchester to Sheffield to see my mum. I used to do my best to bunk off from school on those days, so I could

spend more time with her. This usually involved a tacit relationship with a bottle of Fairy Liquid that I used to drink out
of, and then of course proceed to be violently sick while foam-
ing at the mouth. I don't know just how clued up Mum was at
this stage, but suffice to say I got away with it quite a few times
before I was rumbled.

Nana had been adopted by her mother's sister, as her own
parents couldn't afford to keep her, and grew up through the
Great War in Manchester. I don't know much about her youth,
but I do know in the late twenties she was one of the country's
first lady drivers. (I know this because when I first learned how
to ride a moped she gave me her pair of massive leather
gauntlets she'd used for hand signals so that the male drivers
would be courteous and give way.) She'd had two daughters –
Phyllis and my mum, Betty – with my grandfather, Anthony
Boff. However, through a combination of World War 2 and what
we'll politely call 'Wanderlust', he disappeared. I was only to
meet him once. This was when I was in my early teens, at my
cousin Michael's son's christening. My nana carried on through
the war entertaining the troops with ENSA (Entertainments
National Service Association) and being active with the Civil
Defence, St John's Ambulance Brigade, and the Air Raid Patrol.
She also brought up her two daughters on her own. At seventeen, my Auntie Phyllis became pregnant. The real father long
gone, a man called George married Phyllis and gave my cousin,
Michael John Bishop, his name. From all accounts, Phyllis was a
feisty character. By the time I popped along, her husband had
left and she was a single mum, bringing up Michael on her own,
with my dear nana helping all she could.

During the 1950s, my nana married again – a lovely amateur
musician called Wilfred Arrandale, a warehouseman, and
moved to Denton, Manchester. They didn't have much money;
they didn't even have a fridge. But they did have an outside
loo, in which would be a handbag stuffed with old bits of
rough tissue paper Wilfred had brought home from discarded
packing crates at work. It was all they had. But it did the job.
It was always a jolly household, which we'd visit more or less
every Sunday for tea and fairy cake. Then back we'd go to
Sheffield listening to the Top 30 presented by Alan 'Fluff'

Freeman and then *Sing Something Simple*. Featuring The Mike Sammes Singers, this was a programme dedicated to middle-of-the-road tunes like 'Over the Rainbow'. As soon as we left, Nana and Wilfred would go to their local pub, The Jolly Hatters (Denton was famous for its hat-making industry), for a glass of Mackeson and a Babycham. It wasn't exactly the kind of place where your feet would stick to the carpet, but it wasn't flash either, possessing the mixed aroma of beer, stale tobacco and a hint of 4711 Eau De Toilette. It was their one extravagance, not counting Wilfred's appetite for the gee-gees. Once a week he'd go and place half a crown on some hapless nag in the 4.30 p.m. at Kempton Park.

Auntie Phyllis had been diagnosed with cancer of the womb. Throughout most of her late twenties and early thirties, she bravely fought the disease, finally succumbing to the radiation treatment she received and dying at Christies Hospital, Manchester, in 1963. She had stayed alive just long enough to see her son Mike join the police force. He'd just turned seventeen. She was thirty-four. I remember a neighbour – who had one of the few telephones in our street – coming to the front door to tell Dad the news. When Mum realised what had happened, she was devastated. And as for Nana . . . well, how does a parent cope with their child dying before them?

In later years, Nana lost her beloved Wilfred of a heart attack, and then her eyesight – but she never once lost her courage. Nor did she complain. She was five feet nothing of pure undiluted love, who could express the words *sacrifice* and *selflessness* in a million different ways.

As a little boy, Nana's stories and weekly visits were the highpoint of my life. She was also the first person to encourage me musically. When I was nine I sang on a programme produced by Jess Yates called *Choirs on Sunday*. Subsequently she bought me a diary for my 'Engagements'. This was something she continued to do right up to her death in 1982. She was a character, and even at the age of eighty, when she heard me swear, she'd chase me round the house with her white stick, shaking it at me and shouting, 'You're not too big to be hit!'

I miss her still.

3

HEAVY TIMES

My parents invested a lot of good things in my life, and they meant well. But through a combination of circumstance and genetics their marriage was pre-programmed to implode – and not for want of trying by both parties.

My mum and dad had survived the Blitz, rationing, and all the austerity that World War 2 had brought. They were both from broken families, and yet, when they were young, were filled with all the eternal, spotless optimism of youth. They met, fell in love, got married and jumped on the fifties treadmill of post-war Britain. I came along just a year later. But they were never going to be suited to each other. I knew that – even as a kid.

Apparently, it had all gone horribly wrong when I was six. I remember we had a family holiday to Rhyl in North Wales. I can recall my mum being sad, and my step-grandpa Wilfred playing football with me so I wouldn't get tangled up in what was going on. For many years I thought that this was when Dad told Nana he no longer loved my mum. But it turns out that simply was not true. What *did* happen, though, is that Dad set up a business in Liverpool called Reliance Data Services, and Mum didn't want to move. So from that point on, they effectively led separate lives. Dad worked in Liverpool and came home largely only at weekends until I was sixteen, when they officially separated. So they kind of 'co-existed' for ten years. And they said they did it for me.

Even though I didn't know what was going on, I was pretty disturbed throughout this time. I remember Mum winding me up so much that I threatened her with a knife in front of Nana.

I never did it again. I don't know who was more freaked out – Mum, Nana or me.

At times, hardly surprisingly, the atmosphere in the house was very strained. Two people were living completely separate lives during the week. Then they were thrown together with their son for forty-eight hours at the weekend. Mum and Dad both did their best. I honestly believe that. But it could be a pretty surreal existence. I remember them both arguing at the dinner table on my sixteenth birthday and my quietly asking them to stop, as it was supposed to be a happy day. But again, I'm jumping ahead of myself.

During this long period, I guess both parties must have strayed a little. A couple of images stay with me, such as Mum holding hands with a young cub leader, fifteen years her junior, and my thinking it was a bit weird. However, that was nothing compared to the Scottish holiday I had with her when I was eleven. This extraordinary week remains stamped indelibly on my heart.

Mum and I went to Campbeltown, camping, with the family of one of her scouting friends. Dad didn't come – I suppose he was working. There were two sisters and their husbands, plus their younger, single brother (I'll call him Guy), my mum, and myself. The sisters swapped husbands for the duration of the holiday, and my mum acted like she was married to Guy. All inside two tents. I stuck my head out of the tent one night to see my mum kissing Guy passionately. Why was she doing that? And where was my dad? Confused? Yes, I was. So much for the 'swinging sixties'.

Needless to say, I failed my eleven-plus. I was sent to Tapton Secondary School, but not before my dad fought a valiant rearguard action to try and get me into a grammar school. I was assessed by a friend of the family who was a psychiatrist.

'Nicholas has been very distracted in the last three years,' she said, 'and is, in my opinion, an emotionally disturbed child. Naturally the parents are disappointed, and to some extent, I think, feel responsible.'

Tapton wasn't great. I started off OK in the first year, but basically just ploughed downhill at the beginning of the second until I left. One of my pals back then was Sebastian Coe,

who went on to be one of this country's greatest Olympic ath-
letes – and who even then could run two laps of the 800-metre
track to my one. But there is a more vivid incident on the
sports field that has stayed in my mind.

There was a bully in our class who was determined to make
his mark and show how hard he was. One day, we were all
outside waiting for our games teacher to arrive. Bully Boy
decided to pick on a new lad called Paul. He gave him an
almighty kick in the 'trossachs'. Barely acknowledging what
had happened or the intense pain he must have been feeling,
Paul looked up just as the teacher arrived.

'Now that was an incredibly immature thing to do, wasn't
it?' Paul told Bully Boy.

His adversary was made to look a complete and total idiot
courtesy of self-control and a few well-chosen words. It was a
valuable life lesson for me; my peer had shown awesome self-
control.

For most of my teenage years I came home after school to
the same scene. Mum would generally be in an emotional
state. She would drink sherry first of all. Later she would
'progress' to scotch. She would get me the same tea every
night – cheese on toast with Marmite. And every night I would
sit in front of our coal fire and eat it.

On my own.

At the age of thirteen I had a new problem to contend with.
I developed a stabbing pain in my left testicle. Determined to
try and ignore it, in the hope it would go away, I ploughed on.
But so did the pain. And before long I was lying face down on
the doctor's couch, with what felt like half his hand up my
back passage. I was sent home that night with my eyes water-
ing and a bunch of painkillers. But the next morning, I was
rushed to hospital for an emergency operation – the pain had
grown sharp and intense like a knife that went right through
me. I felt like I was receiving 5,000 volts. It turned out I had a
growth on my left testicle that looked suspicious.

They operated and found it was all twisted. The lump
turned out to be a cyst of the epidymis and was, thank God,
benign. But my left testicle now resembled something that
Jonny Wilkinson might kick – and was approximately the

same size! So I was sent to Ryegate Children's Annexe to recuperate. I was given a metal cage to lift the sheets and blankets off my painful parts.

The nurses were lovely and one in particular was very pretty. I struggled with my thirteen-year-old thought-life and prayed my stitches wouldn't burst, while thanking God on a daily basis for the metal frame that kept any further embarrassment out of sight. Being a teenager is confusing enough. But when my dad inadvertently let slip to one of my schoolmates what kind of operation I'd had, well let's just say I've had happier times. It was character building, to say the least.

At some point in my teens I started to form a very basic kind of faith. I had no problem believing in heaven, or that Jesus died for the mistakes I made. So, purely based on head knowledge, I decided to get confirmed in the Church of England. On the day in question, I went forward for the Bishop of Sheffield to bless me with the 'laying on of hands'.

I remember I felt a warmth and peace flow through me. It started at my head and slowly flooded every part of my body. And with it came such incredible serenity. It was my first tangible experience of God, and I guess it formed the foundation for my future spiritual development. The form of language used in the service might just as well have been ancient Greek – I didn't understand any of it. But the feeling in my heart and my soul was totally real and authentic.

My parents' response to my confirmation was the gift of a silver cross bearing the date (30 April 1972), a pewter tankard, and a gold fountain pen. There was a party attended by Nana and husband Wilfred, Dad, and my mum – who got blitzed.

I remember Friday nights when Mum used to go to the jazz club at The Norfolk Arms. Before they split up, my dad would go along, too. I would be smuggled in, given a bag of Bovril crisps and a glass of Vimto and I'd quietly sit in the corner watching Big Al and his band play tunes like 'Chime Blues'. Mum would enjoy the company of her mates and get smashed most times we went.

Still, I loved the sights, sounds and smells that I found there. Somehow it was comforting. I remember the clarinettist took a shine to me. Occasionally I'd go round to his house to improvise on my violin, trying to play along with whatever tune he was blowing. My plan back then was to play jazz violin like Stephane Grappelli, who was my hero. It didn't quite pan out like that, though.

Anyway, with Guy – Mum's boyfriend on the holiday from hell – on the scene now, it was agreed that she should have complete freedom to see him, but not in the family home. For a couple of years this is what happened until I turned sixteen. A date was set for my parents to separate – 1 September 1973. I don't blame Mum and Dad. We're all human and I loved them, but it wasn't easy.

Sadly, I think Mum really believed she'd marry Guy, and they tried hard to make it work. But it didn't. What was promised was never delivered, and Mum was never to find real happiness again.

At least, not on this earth.

4

GLITTERING STARDOM

One of the redeeming features of my teens was my violin teacher David Adams, who was the leader of the South Yorkshire Symphony Orchestra. He was an amazing man who could make his fiddle laugh, cry and talk – sometimes all in the space of a few bars of music. I used to walk a mile or two to his bungalow and have my lessons with him every Saturday morning at eleven o'clock.

He was an inspiring and passionate man who believed in my abilities from the word 'go' and a great, if tough, teacher. If he was pleased he'd playfully cuff me round the back of the head. If he was disappointed then he'd remain silent and I would know that I'd hurt him. Even then, I knew I was blessed to be given the opportunity to study with him.

When I first met David, I burst into tears. My first violin teacher was retiring and moving away; I was upset about this, perhaps because I needed a male figure in my life to compensate for my father's absences. Anyway, when David asked me to play, I refused, and cried.

'I will take him because he has real emotion,' said David, even though I hadn't played a single note.

For a time I became lead violinist with the Sheffield Youth Orchestra. However, I wasn't content with the violin, and became desperate for a guitar. Mum and Dad were cool with this, and so the deal was if I passed my grade five violin exam, I could have a classical guitar. I scraped through with 104 marks out of 120. A pass was 100.

My favourite teacher at Tapton was Jim Vickers. He was very hard, but fair, and taught me technical drawing. He used to call me 'Nickel-Arse'. But I developed my own response to his cheek.

'Actually, sir, it's chromium-plated,' I said with temerity.

'I make the jokes round here, Battle – not you!' he said, clipping me round the ear.

When I finally told him about my parents, he became a rock for me in my final year. His was one of the few subjects I passed. In fact, I got a grade one CSE.

So when I left Tapton, I had three 'O' levels – music, technical drawing and French. I'd failed everything else including English. Once again Dad lobbied the school system so that I could try and retake my missing 'O' levels while studying for my 'A' levels. But it was not to be. Despite my father's attempts to defeat the establishment, I went to King Edward VII School, known locally as 'King Ted's', where I was plonked in to the sixth form (Removed) which is where they put all the difficult kids like me.

If I remember rightly, I managed to squeeze another couple of 'O' levels out while I was at King Ted's. I even passed English – even though I was still in bed when the exam started! I arrived half an hour late, but my year tutor, who had rung me at home to remind me, allowed me to sit the paper. I repeated the same trick for history – but failed that. I can remember being so bored with the whole exam process that when given a multi-choice paper I simply created symmetrical designs on the paper. Unsurprisingly, I failed that, too. I think it was maths.

Speech Day came around. It was held at the 3,000-seater Sheffield City Hall. I led the school orchestra. I also performed two songs with my own ensemble – my own composition titled 'Remnants', and James Taylor's 'Fire and Rain', one of my favourite songs of all time. My parents were sitting opposite each other in the balcony – my dad with the new lady in his life, Verlon, and my mum with her best friend and drinking partner. As I stood up to begin my performance, the 'E' string on my violin snapped.

'Can you please just bear with me while I restring?' I told the audience. I chatted to them for a minute or two, then proceeded to perform the two songs. We received an amazing response.

'A distinguished contribution to prize-giving,' is how my teacher described my performance.

My dad told me recently it was that point in time he realised that whatever happened, I had the confidence to survive. It might have been obvious to him, but it was to elude me for many years to come.

Dad's life started to come together when he met and later married my step-mum, Verlon. She first came into our lives along with her first husband when Dad and he worked together at NCR in Division Street, Sheffield. Dad, and possibly Mum, had become godparents to their kids, Lynne and Catherine. Later, after getting into severe financial difficulties – and probably a whole load else I knew nothing about – Verlon and her husband split up. Verlon was left to look after the girls on her own. Dad used to pop round from time to time and take the girls out, to give her a break.

One day, after he had dropped them back home, the two of them kissed. From that point on, they were inseparable. Dad had found his soul mate at last. (They married on 11 August 1977, and I was their best man. It was strange, watching my dad marry someone other than my mum, and stranger still to be presented with two stepsisters.)

Verlon was always *much* more than 'just' a step-mum, even though I could be very difficult in my teens. Once through the 'teenage stuff', I came to think of her like a big sister, but also a very good friend. She was instrumental in my life in so many ways, including helping me find our first family home in Chorleywood and introducing me to her friend Cynthia's daughter. But that's another story.

When Mum first heard about Dad and Verlon getting together, she was apoplectic. She made it very difficult for me to go and see them. She succeeded in making me feel incredibly guilty for doing so. I guess this isn't unusual when a couple splits up and there are children involved. The kids can end up as 'Piggy in the middle'. Here's an extract from a letter I wrote at the time to my dad, which I'm amazed he kept.

For the time being I can't see you anymore, while Verlon is at Commonside. I can't really go there. You've no idea of the home situation here, to be told that I'm despised by Mum and C [her best friend], to my face for seeing you and Verlon . . . and little things the kids have said have stuck in my throat. I'm choked and . . . fed up. I don't know what to do anymore . . . Mum told me she believes I'm the drug-taking type. Apparently ALL pop stars are . . .

So my naked ambition to join a band was obvious even to my mum . . .

The summer after I started at King Ted's, I took my first guitar on holiday with my dad to Menorca. On the second night I met a chap called Sam who owned a bar and who had released a record in the sixties. I ended up playing there every night (sixteen of 'em!) until, sadly, it was time to go home. We used to sing Jose Feliciano songs and I learned a little bit of Flamenco from him.

We used to have this routine where we'd play our guitars very quickly, shout 'Olé!' toss them up in the air so they'd spin through 360°, knock them in the back and carry on playing, without missing a beat. On a good night this worked a treat. However, if you'd had one too many bevvies then it could be carnage as the guitar would come crashing down amid all the glasses. It was good fun. But I'd rather stick pins in my eyes than have to sing 'Viva Espana' again!

It was in Menorca that I discovered for the first time that my dad could be my friend and to this day he remains so. To his credit he never patronised me, and from my late teens onwards was always there if ever life with my mum became too much. I think he recognised then, as he does now, that my childhood wasn't easy, and I have to say that for all the difficult times we've had, he's still my dad, he's my mate and I love him.

After the summer break I went back to school to study for my 'A' levels. What a joke. I ended up taking *four* 'A' levels. How daft was that! It had taken me two attempts to get five 'O' levels! I got thrown out of French because the secondary system had left me so far behind I could never catch up with my tenses. I had to give up Music, because we didn't have a piano and how was I ever going to achieve grade five standard in a year? That left me with Divinity (religious studies) and English Literature. I duly failed both.

It wasn't all bad, though. I became a prefect, ran the Entertainments Committee, and had time to grow up and be mentored a little by a great teacher called Jack North. Oh yes – and I did have lots of fun. I joined various school bands. Eclipse was my first, where I was rapidly fired as a drummer and ended up as the lead singer. We played one memorable gig at what was then a dodgy Hell's Angels pub called the Minerva Tavern in the centre of Sheffield.

We did cover versions of seventies rock classics like 'Smoke on the Water' by Deep Purple and 'All Right Now' by Free. Somehow we survived, and were each paid the princely sum of 50p. I gave my money to my mum, as it was my first income ever from music. Years later I was going through some stuff of hers, and found a pencil rubbing of it. Written at the bottom in turquoise ink it said, 'Nick's first wages from music.' So she had been proud of me after all. As I realised this, too late, water rose in my eyes.

Just before they separated, my parents had bought me a gift. It was red and silver, and looked incredibly cool. And with two people on the back of it, the thing would ascend a hill as fast as a very old Qualcast motorised lawnmower. But it brought me independence. The Mobylette Sports Moped – now a recognised classic(!).

Dad had insisted I take the RAC/ACU training scheme before being allowed on the road, which was a sound idea, as it gave me a head start when it came to my driving test. I had the coolest lime green crash helmet with matching visor. I thought I was the mutt's nuts. The only problem was, after my parents had split up and Dad was with Verlon, every time I left the house, my mother would accuse me of going to see my dad, and proceed to give me a hard time.

Sometimes I did go. Sometimes I didn't. I did my best to conceal it, so as not to hurt her. Now and again, though, I'd get caught out and that would just undermine things further. Mum did her best to be supportive, but I think her own life was so difficult for her; she struggled sometimes just to get through the day. Night after night I'd come home from school to find her and her best friend drinking scotch and discussing the meaning of life. The more they drank the more vociferous and argumentative they became.

I used to travel miles on my moped. With my jumbo acoustic guitar strapped to my back, I'd wobble all over Sheffield. I was forever getting stopped by the police. But my parents never knew, and to be honest I didn't give a monkey's.

By the way, I only fell off the moped once. But in fairness, I was fighting through a blizzard and I couldn't see anything. Remember David Essex singing 'Silver Dream Machine'? Well, that was my funky moped – all 49ccs of her.

I started going to Crusaders, a youth-club-come-Bible-class. It was here that I first met Georgina and Helen, with whom I formed Namesake. We were a kind of gospel-folk group playing the local church circuit, and on occasions the Highcliffe Arms Folk Club. At the club, I blagged us our first gig supporting John James, the brilliant ragtime guitarist. He was particularly kind to me, and wrote me a note that said, 'Keep playing your own stuff!' It was Sheffield's best and most popular folk club and was typically populated by an assortment of bearded people wearing interesting cardigans and rolling their own cigarettes or smoking pipes while they supped their pints of Ward's best bitter. And that was just the girls.

I liked hanging out with Georgina and Helen. Georgina's parents Mr and Mrs Sear were always very kind to me. I secretly harboured 'thoughts' about both girls. But Georgina was going out with one of my pals, Richard and, apart from the occasional stolen kiss, I don't think Helen was very interested in me.

The peak of our endeavours was when we hired Sheffield's 500-seater Memorial Hall, promoted our own concert ably abetted by my friends Richard and Fran Morrison, from the YMCA – and sold the thing out! We were reviewed in the *Star*, Sheffield's local paper, and for all of a week I felt dead famous! I loved it. In fact, I have to say that my overriding talent back then was not musical, but a tenacious desire to succeed almost at any cost. I had chips firmly balanced on both shoulders.

Through the YMCA, Richard and Fran provided a safe place for dysfunctional little basket cases like me to offload their problems while also encouraging us with our talents and talking to us about God. Through a contact of his called Dave Ling, Richard got me in the studio, arranged a session for us at BBC Radio Sheffield, and was an incredible help and encouragement to me in my early years.

It was Richard who promoted a show for the Nick Battle Band at the YMCA, which featured – among others – a young Matthew Bannister. He was a featured vocalist, resplendent in mascara and make-up, doing his own inimitable rendition of 'Hold Back the Night' (originally by The Trammps but Matthew's delivery was more akin to Graham Parker's version). This was, of course, long before he became head of BBC Radio.

Also in the audience, heckling, and being his usual loud and colourful self, was Bruce Dickinson – for the last twenty years or so lead singer of Iron Maiden. I really liked Bruce. We hooked up a couple of times; first when he was in the eighties rock band Samson, and then in the early days of Iron Maiden.

The last time I saw him, though, we were both at a post-Ivor Novello Awards do (the Ivors are the songwriting equivalent of the Oscars). I was struggling with life and more than a little worse for wear, and he was still his ebullient self. He's still singing with Iron Maiden, and I believe still fencing (he's an excellent swordsman), and is presently also involved with a music college in Brighton, as one of their key supporters and lecturers.

Before I end this chapter, I must add a postscript to my time at King Ted's. This is my last report from the deputy headmaster. He wrote

'July fast approaches, Nick cannot enter a fantasy world of glittering stardom that does not exist.'

Yeah, right.

5

VINYL MATTERS

My 'holy grail' was black vinyl. And it had a hole in the middle. In the summer of 1976, I'd finally left school, and I was determined to make my grand entrance into the music business. I'd written to a bunch of record stores in the area and had managed to get a meeting with the owner of one of them.

'Go and stand by the fridges in Marks and Sparks before you go in for your interview,' Mum said.

It was good advice. I arrived for my interview at Bradley's Records, on time and nicely chilled out. The shop back then was located at the top of Fargate in Sheffield, and had been kitted out with all the modern gear you needed. It wasn't as cool as Virgin Records' new store, but it was the closest thing to the music biz that I could find back then.

So, I was going to start my career in music, selling records for one of the north's key independent record store owners, Mr Bradley of Bradley's Records. He was a nice man who gave me the opportunity to go to college one day a week to learn about retail management. (Incidentally, I came top in two subjects on the course – display and law. Go figure.)

Even then, the writing was on the wall – with the balance of creativity and commerce which has now become part of my trade. I love to create. But I also love to cut a deal. I guess it's the mixture of Mum, the sensitive artist, and my dad, the pragmatic businessman.

Anyway, I started off at the Fargate Branch, before being moved to Bradley's Chapel Walk shop. I was allowed 22.5 per cent discount off any records I purchased, and at my discretion was allowed to give discount to my family and friends as well.

The only problem was this went a little too well. Half my mates from my old school, King Ted's, came in to buy their records from me – with the result that the shop's profits took a significant downturn for a month or so until they worked out what was going on! I got a stiff talking-to by the shop manageress, whose name escapes me but whose face never will.

I was moved to Bradley's quietest shop where the owner's son also worked. He was a top bloke and, like me, trying to find his way. I ended up having a great time with him, each of us turning the other on to some new and exciting band or record. It was fun and I soaked up all the music like a sponge. But I wasn't really going anywhere.

In the August of that year, I wangled some holiday time. My friend from the local Crusader class, Pete Williams, told me all about a Christian music festival called Greenbelt where they had fantastic bands and you could get to know more about God. To be honest, the latter didn't hold much appeal for me back then, but I was definitely up for checking out the music.

So off we went – and had a wonderful if extremely wet weekend. While there, I managed to meet Bryn Haworth, whose band headlined on the Saturday night and who blew everybody else away. Bryn is one of the greatest slide guitarists this country has ever produced, and has played on a number of albums by classic artists from Joan Armatrading to Gerry Rafferty.

'I want to do what you do,' I told him. 'Can you please help me?'

I managed to get his address and he became a mentor and a source of great encouragement to me. Thirty years later, Bryn remembers seeing in me someone 'just as lost as I had been'. I think that was why he tried to help me.

A month or so after Greenbelt, I thanked Mr Bradley very much for the opportunity and the job, then resigned. In one momentary lapse of reason, I went to work for my dad for all of three months. He had a business called Reliance Computer Group, who specialised in buying and selling second-hand computer systems. What possessed me, I don't know.

I bought a blue pinstripe suit and did my best to look like a salesman. But I wasn't cut out to follow my father's dream and work with him in the business. Also, being the boss' son, if I did something wrong – like the time I crashed the car in a snowstorm – I always got more of a bawling out than anybody else.

There were some colourful characters that passed through the trade. Like Fred, who would always try and ply me with gin and tonic by the bucket load whenever we met at business dos. He turned out to be just about in the closet and a con man wanted by several agencies for leaving debts all over the globe. His CV apparently ranked up there as one of the greatest works of fiction since Chaucer's *Canterbury Tales*.

Dad wanted me to go to night school to take business studies. I was reluctant, as it meant less time to devote to my music. It proved to be a tipping point for me.

On 17 January 1977, I saw American blue-eyed soul singers Daryl Hall and John Oates perform on the Bigger Than Both of Us tour at Sheffield's City Hall. This local venue was where all the big groups came to play. It was a grand building of classical revival style, constructed in the 1930s with huge pillars at the front and steps leading up to the entrance. Many of the great names from the entertainment world of the twentieth century have played there.

My mates and I always used to get to the City Hall early. We'd pile down the front before the gig started, to look at all the gear on the stage. We would nod sagely to each other about the size of the bass drum or how big the lead guitarist's Marshall stack amplifier was. When Hall and Oates came on stage looking impossibly glamorous and sang the coolest harmonies I had ever heard, I was hooked.

'If I can achieve just some of what they have done, then I've got to do it,' I said to myself.

That was it. The next day I went in and resigned from my dad's company. He wasn't thrilled. He must have wondered what on earth was going to happen to me. He got all official and wrote me a letter accepting my resignation, and said that in time I could have made a good salesman. He also told me that I was on my own, and that it was up to me to make it work. Only later did I discover that he secretly guaranteed my overdraft while I got myself sorted. Tough love.

So I drifted around for about three months. Then just as I was despairing of ever getting into the music business, I heard that the Christian rock band After the Fire were looking for a bass player. The band had been going for a couple of years, born out of two acts – a progressive rock band called Narnia which Peter Banks had been in, and a folk duo called Ishmael and Andy, which gave them the inimitable Andy Piercy.

They had started to cross over and play secular gigs. The bass player, Robin Childs, had just left the band. The sound was a hybrid between progressive rock groups like ELP, Yes and Genesis, complicated structures and time signatures that tested one's musical metal.

Undeterred by the fact that I couldn't play bass at this point and my faith was pretty thin, I sent them a hastily recorded demo from a session at the local YMCA four-track studio. I included a photo of me with my electric guitar – an Antoria gold top Les Paul copy.

To my complete amazement, they responded.

6

AFTER THE FIRE

So, After the Fire wanted to see me! But I didn't have enough money to get down to Colchester where the band were based. So I decided to hitch. However, that day, Richard and Fran Morrison, my dear friends from the local YMCA, rang up.

'Somebody has left an envelope at reception for you,' they said. 'Do you want to pick it up before you leave Sheffield?'

I said goodbye to Verlon – Dad was away in Holland on business at the time – and went down to the YMCA to collect my post. It contained enough cash to buy me a return ticket to Colchester . . . with just enough left over for a copy of the music paper *Sounds*, and a cup of coffee.

On the way down I read and re-read the tiny paragraph about former bass player Robin Childs leaving the band. I dreamed that maybe I might get the gig. I met Andy Piercy, Pete Banks and Ian Adamson that day. They gave me an orange Fender Musicmaster bass to play, and we went through some pretty complicated stuff together.

'Look, I've come a long way,' I said at the end of it. 'I would love to join your band. Am I in?'

Andy asked me to leave the room. A few minutes later they all summoned me back in.

'Yes,' they said.

I went ballistic, leaping up and down, hugging them all. I was like Tigger in one of A.A. Milne's books; I just wouldn't stop jumping around. All that I'd dreamed of was about to come true. I was going to be – no, I was the bass player in After the Fire, also known as ATF to their fans.

ATF fans were among some of the most fanatical, loyal and loving people you could ever hope to meet. They would wear open-toed leather sandals which we nicknamed 'Palestine pit-boots', and would frequently carry a leather-bound Bible, while wearing the ATF logo T-shirt from the album *Signs of Change*. They were a joy to behold – and still are. There was only one real drawback with them, as far as the owners of the pubs and clubs were concerned. Like us, they would only ever drink pints of orange juice!

I went home on the train that day, excitedly told Verlon the news, and started packing. A couple of days later, she kindly drove down with me to Harwich where we picked up my dad off the ferry before dropping me at Fox House, in a little village called Langham on the outskirts of Colchester, where Pete and Charlotte Banks lived. That was to be my home for the next few weeks. I kissed Dad and Verlon goodbye. And my adventure began.

It was 30 April 1977. Punk was about to explode. As for me, I'd joined a Christian progressive rock band, but I couldn't really play the bass . . . and my faith in God was pretty thin. Hmmm . . . just where would I go from here?

I rehearsed solidly with the band for about ten days. Then we went straight into a 26-date tour of the United Kingdom. We visited every toilet imaginable. You name it, we seemed to play it. You might have been there (check the appendix at the end of this story to find out the full list of dates and venues – direct from my diary!).

We seemed to follow The Stranglers around. They were one of the darker and more controversial bands of the 'new wave' era. Quite a contrast. We ended up playing the same venues that they had played the previous night, all over the country. The week we headlined the legendary Marquee in London, Squeeze played the night before and The Police played the night after. So we were in good company.

We were not helped by the fact that our agent obviously had an extremely tenuous grasp of geography when it came to tour dates. For example, when you live in Colchester, a one-off gig in Lytham St Annes is a massive commitment.

We'd get up and load the van. Three lucky people would sit in the front. Two unlucky ones would have to sit in the back with the gear in a windowless aluminium box, munching on carbon monoxide from the leaky exhaust. Dave Cooke, initially our sole roadie/soundman and really the fifth member of the band, would drive us sometimes hundreds of miles.

On arrival, we'd unload the gear, and hump it into the club – sometimes in precarious circumstances. Take a bow The Lion, Warrington, with its rusty fire escape. Then there was Plymouth Woods Club. If you stamped your foot on the stage, the power would go off. Stamp it again and it would surge back on, often with interesting results.

Before the gig, we might have time to throw down a Chinese takeaway, quickly change and perform for an hour and a bit. Sometimes we'd play to punters who adored us; often, to the gloriously indifferent. We'd then pack down and drive home, get to bed between twelve and two in the morning, get up at eight or nine and repeat the process all over again. I was 'fit as a butcher's dog'. (Oh, to have that body now!) But do you know what? I look back on those times with Andy, Pete, Ian and then Ivor, and our manager Jonathan Cooke, with tremendous affection.

I was the youngest in the band, having just left school the previous summer. Andy and Pete wrote all the songs. They were hard taskmasters. Back then Andy was a perfectionist, and at times could be quite stern. He was – and still is – a complete star. In later years he became a sought-after producer, and one of this country's most influential worship leaders.

There is one incident that sticks in my mind. We had this song called 'Dance of the Marionette', during which at one point Andy would imitate a puppet having its strings pulled. One night while doing his routine at The Stapleton Tavern in Crouch End, a bored, inebriated female punter wandered straight up to him and unzipped his flies. Bless him. He didn't blink, but we all collapsed laughing.

I've got loads of good memories of this time. Once, we'd driven all the way to Bradford from Colchester to play at the Princeville Working Men's Club. Let me put it politely. We 'died'. You could hear a pin drop as we walked offstage.

'Playing your music here, is like trying to take a flying ****
at a rolling doughnut,' said the club manager. 'Here's your
money, now piss off home.'

I guess he was never going to get a job in the diplomatic
corps – but we were never going to play there again!

Pete was the businessman. Creative yet technical, he
devised and built, with help from Dave Cooke, our PA system
– and created a company called Epicentrum. He had a massive
Hammond organ and Leslie cabinet. I loved the sound of this
gear, but grew to hate it as we lugged it up and down everywhere. Pete also had a great musical brain and was responsible for ATF's trademark keyboard sound which the American
rock group Van Halen were later to emulate so cleverly for
their hit 'Jump'.

Ian Adamson was the brilliant drummer in the band and
became my mentor and hero for a while. I lived for a time with
him and his parents Mattie and Dave in Harold Hill, Essex.
They were truly wonderful to me. Ian encouraged and nur-
tured my music and my tenuous walk with God. For a while,
he was the older brother I'd never had. But shortly after I
joined the band, he left. No, it wasn't because of me – more
because he'd fallen in love with a beautiful Californian girl. He
now lives in the USA and is involved working with people
with mental health issues and heads up a big department
funded by the state.

Ivor Twiddle replaced Ian on the drums. Can you imagine
having a rhythm section called Battle & Twiddle? In later
years, Ivor changed his name to Iva Twydell (to avoid confu-
sion?!). Now he's a highly ranked policeman somewhere in
Bedfordshire. He was also a larger-than-life character, a gentle
giant with a great sense of humour. I went on to be involved in
both his solo records, *Waiting for the Son*, on which I played fiddle pretty terribly and also sang some backing vocals, and his
later album *Duel*. I produced the latter with my friend
Anthony Phillips, a founding member of the rock group
Genesis.

The highlight of my time with ATF was headlining
Greenbelt in 1977. In later years, U2 and Runrig were to play
at this increasingly popular Christian arts festival. Back then, I

guess you could say we were all pioneers. The year before I'd
been as a punter with my pal, Pete Williams. Now I was playing at Greenbelt – and we were top of the bill.

I loved it. I ran around the stage like Sebastian Coe on the
tail of Steve Ovett. It was great. As I look back over the last fifty
years, it is still one of those highlights that you tend to replay
in your imagination. I played my violin, and as we performed
'Jigs' from our debut album *Signs of Change*, I had to dodge the
hail of coins as people lobbed money onto the stage. We were
so hard up those days, we picked up *all* the coins afterwards.
Living largely by faith our staple diet was eggy bread.

Looking back now, I realise just how extremely blessed I was
to even be in that situation. And we had the best part of 20,000
people going crazy as we played. That experience probably
comes a close second to making love. (Maybe not *that* close!)

During this time I moved in with a lovely Christian family,
the Farrows. They let me live with them more or less rent free
as long as I helped occasionally with the work they would get
in from the local electronics factory, to help earn a little extra
cash. How they put up with me, I don't know. I'm just grateful
they did. It was the beginning of many extravagant examples
of selfless Christian love I would experience in my lifetime.

Roundabout December of 1977, I began to feel a bit disillu-
sioned musically with the band. It didn't seem we were getting
anywhere quick enough. I was also very young, hopelessly
immature and beginning to get a little arrogant. Sure, we'd
made our own album, had been played on Radio 1 by Alan
'Fluff' Freeman and Annie Nightingale – and I think even John
Peel. But at that point it seemed I could have more fun if I
joined a more colourful, liberal and exciting bunch of musicians called Fish Co.

So I left ATF. It didn't help that Bev, one of the lead vocalists
in Fish Co, was the cousin of Andy's wife Judy. I acted entirely
in my own self-interest, without thinking of the consequences
for the others, and although I did return to the band for a one-
off gig at Strathclyde University, Glasgow, to help them out, that
was it.

I acted like a prat. I've obviously since apologised. But let's
be honest, my leaving didn't exactly hold them back. Andy

and Pete started writing pop songs – strangely enough, something I wanted them to do – and went on to have massive hit records in Canada, the USA, and South Africa.

My favourite song from ATF? I have two – 'Now That I've Found' from *Signs of Change* and a later track 'One Rule For You'. The former always moved me emotionally when we played it live – it had a great sense of rebirth and God about it. The latter is one of the greatest pop songs ever written, and still largely an undiscovered gem.

By the way, I got my first royalty cheque from After the Fire just the other day – twenty-nine years later. It was for the princely sum of £50.03.

And do you know what? It felt great.

7

FISH IN DEEP WATER

He held the world record for hypnotising chickens. He was one of the most charismatic, funny, artistic, multi-talented, extraordinarily skilled, spiritual and creative people I'd ever met. Stephen Angus Fairnie was a graduate of the Royal College of Art, a painter, sculptor, songwriter, vocalist, husband to Bev, later a father to Famie and Jake, and an inventor – along with Pete 'Willie' Williams – of the board game Hype.

He was as mad as I was. Yet different. It was perfect.

Steve and Bev seemed to be the perfect couple, artistic, articulate, and attractive. Fairnie's other partner in life was his best mate Steve Rowles, with whom he wrote all the songs and shared, along with Bev, the vocal duties. There was another glorious eccentric character on lead guitar called Jules Hardwick. The son of Mollie Hardwick, writer of *Upstairs, Downstairs*, he had previously played in the seventies rock band Curved Air. I thought he was cool.

So I joined this motley crew. Then we hired a drummer called Steve 'Urry Up Arry 'Axell. Arry lived his life at a speed which was the polar opposite of mine. When it came to drumming, he had two speeds – slow and stop. When it came to playing bass, I was like a greyhound let out of the trap sprinting away like a mad thing. It didn't make for a very tight rhythm section, but it was a laugh.

This was Fish Co. They were an eccentric and colourful collective, not unlike the off-beat seventies band Deaf School. Quirky, opinionated – and certainly not to everyone's taste – we had a great deal of fun and tried not to offend too many people. But we did push boundaries! If the twelve disciples had gone to the Royal College of Art, they might have become similar fishers of men.

We were a merry, dysfunctional band of Christians who truly loved each other, and had some very funny times together. Frequently we'd have to pull on to the hard shoulder of the motorway in our slate-grey Transit van. Rowles, who always drove, would be laughing so much that we were in danger of crashing. The whole van would shake until we regained our composure.

Fairnie always had his own special armchair in the van from which he would dispense his anecdotes and observations, keeping us all entertained. Jules would have his lips locked on to a No. 6 cigarette. I would normal be chastising Arry, arguably the most conservative of the group. Bev would be mother hen but also fiercely protective of her man, and Rowles would have his eyes fixed on to the endless grey ribbon that stretched ahead of us.

We were all desperate to be pop stars. We soon changed our name to Writz, got a manager, secured a record deal and then found ourselves in the studio with Godley and Creme from 10cc.

It was here, for me, that the wheels started to fall off the bus.

Day one at Essex Studios in Poland Street, Godley and Creme arrived with their engineer. They proceeded to rip out the monitors before we did anything. Their engineer had just been working with The Police, who were one of the coolest bands at the time, and Godley and Creme were my heroes. I was both intimidated and determined to try and be at the top of my game throughout the session.

They had had shed-loads of hits as part of the group 10cc. Only a few years before, at the end of our school dance, I'd held a lovely girl called Sue close as their hit 'I'm Not in Love' was played. (They, of course, turned out to be exactly right.)

Then somebody turned up in the studio and opened up an attaché case.

'What's that you got there?' someone else asked.

'Oh, there's some Colombian marching powder, some Moroccan black, a little Lebanese red and some Thai sticks,' said the person with the case.

Some of my mates around school had allegedly taken acid. But I'd never been around drugs of an illegal kind before. Still, I was used to people being out of control because I'd grown up with my mum and alcohol. Secretly, deep down – possibly through learned behaviour – I wanted to be out of control, too.

I soon got the opportunity. I'd made a pact with one of my girlfriends that neither of us would try drugs. We pledged to 'stay pure'. But at a party given by a fan of the band in his Earl's Court pad, I spotted my pal gently hoovering up a line of cocaine. I'd had just enough wine to salve any conscience.

'Stuff it,' I said to myself, 'I'll have some, too.'

The first time was incredible. But as ever with any drug, the novelty or effect soon wore off. The temporary euphoria and high made me feel confident, powerful and very much in control. It's the perfect lie. The complete opposite is true. You can quickly become diffident, insecure and incoherent. On occasion, while with the band, I would take it before gigs, sometimes even before going into the studio in the morning. I had bought the rock 'n' roll lie: 'Live fast, die young, and have a good-looking corpse.'

My band-mates knew little about my extremes. During this time, I felt so low, so worthless. I felt I'd turned my back on God for a potential fleeting five minutes of fame. To die would have been a good result. My early life had come back to haunt me. Deep down I knew I was nothing. I tortured myself with the thought that the 'Jesus thing' had been all right, but it wasn't how the *real world* lived. After all, I figured, Mum was 'a Christian', wasn't she? And a fat lot of good it was doing her.

'Stuff it,' I thought.

I was a failed Christian with a fickle heart. Just where would this lead me? Whenever I was around 'controlled substances' and felt the desire to imbibe whatever was on offer, I would have this fractured internal dialogue going on inside my head:

'Go on, do it, do it, it doesn't matter. Enjoy yourself.'

'Don't do it! You're worth more.'

And finally, 'Do it anyway – who cares?'

Most times, the darkness won.

I was with the band at a pub in Wardour Street, Soho, London. I think it was someone's birthday. Anyway we started drinking, and for some reason I decided that Pernod was going to be my weapon of choice for the evening. I proceeded to get very, very drunk. In fact, I was legless. I think Rowles (always reliable) carried me down the street to an office.

I woke the next morning, not knowing where I was, to find somebody saying to me, 'Listen man, I really like you, and my girlfriend really likes you, and if ever you know, you wanna, you know, it would be cool with me, I wouldn't mind, and she'd love it.'

I fled the building. I virtually crawled home to Finchley, where I was crashing on a friend of a friend's floor, drank a litre of orange juice and passed out. During this time I also managed to get engaged to a nurse who was a lovely soul, but I was a mess and not in a fit state to marry anybody. We broke up, and I have to say it was my fault. She came from a lovely Christian family who were always very accepting towards me. Years later, through a mutual and painful journey, we got in touch again, and I was able to apologise. But back then, all I was concerned with was, 'doh, ray, me, me, me'.

The year 1979 was tough. We seemed to be touring Holland almost constantly, to no effect. We had badges made saying, 'The wages of sin are £10 per week and £6 a gig' – and still we never got paid.

I remember one time arriving at a club in Amsterdam called The Milky Way, also known locally as De Melkweg. I'd never seen a place like it before. To make matters more interesting, though, for once we had actually received six weeks' backlog of wages from our management.

The venue had a reputation as being a bit of a hippy joint, but seemed friendly enough. So as soon as I got my money, I rushed into the canteen, bought myself a bottle of wine and a cake, and sat there happily for a while eating and feeling 'full' for the first time in weeks. Suddenly my legs turned to jelly, my brain to liquid goo and the room began to spin. I giggled uncontrollably.

The cake was laced with hashish.

Worse still, Mark Ellen from the *New Musical Express* had travelled to Amsterdam to interview us, and was then going to come on the road with us to Paris for our show there. I don't remember much of the gig. The next thing I knew, it was about five o'clock in the morning and we were at a service station in Lille, Northern France. I was doing my best to impersonate the 'Knights Who Like To Say Ni' from *Monty Python and the Holy Grail*. I made Humpty Dumpty look together. Apparently, Mark Ellen had driven most of the way.

From Lille we made it to Paris, where Steve Jones from The Sex Pistols turned up at our gig. A lot of alcohol was consumed. I would like to say we had a deep and meaningful conversation about the future of rock 'n' roll. However back then, deep down I was shallow and probably more concerned about trying to get some publicity. Still, from what I can remember, Steve seemed to be a very nice chap.

We ended up with this massive crowd of people wandering round trying to get a drink, but the Parisians were wise to our ways and declined to let our party in to their establishments. From Paris we drove down to Lyon where we played a great gig. But the promoter had booked us into a whorehouse. Worse still, there weren't enough bedrooms.

Pete Williams and I bolted for the first available room we could find – and barricaded ourselves in. The beds were as damp as a lettuce patch. The room was just above Lyon's mainline railway station. I've slept better. But at least what little virtue that I had left remained intact that night.

We released one single in France on Barclay Records called 'Movies'. That sank without trace. We also toured Germany. It was a lot of fun, but a shambles. At the end of the year, everything just seemed to crash down around me. The record company went belly-up, we had no money, I was homeless; I had taken to sleeping on anyone's floor that would let me. I lived out of an old grey suitcase that used to belong to my mum, with the legend 'Writz' sprayed on it in black paint. Most of my world was contained in it.

I was beyond depressed. I didn't care what happened to me. I just wanted to be safe. I guess that I was hanging on by a fingernail to any kind of existence. But ultimately I felt completely wretched.

One evening I ended up at Westminster Chapel, which a couple of my more responsible Christian mates had told me about, and where Dr R.T. Kendall was the pastor. In need of tea and biscuits, I met a bloke called Trevor Von Trilsbach, a reformed skinhead, who'd become an insurance salesman. He offered me his sofa to sleep on until I got myself sorted. He gave me £20 a week, took me out on a Friday for a pizza and began to remind me of God. He wanted nothing in return. His faith humbled me then, and it humbles me now. Where would I have been without that simple act of love?

Christmas 1979 I left the band, went back to Sheffield, and started to try and piece my pathetic little life together. But what would it take?

8

THE POSTMAN ALWAYS SINGS TWICE

I was in poor shape. Physically, the road had taken its toll. Mentally, I was groaning under the weight of a sense of failure. But I was happy to have a roof over my head, and to get regular meals while I stayed with Dad and Verlon.

I saw my mum. I confessed to her what a mess I'd made of everything. I confessed to God while sitting on a gravestone at Christchurch, where I'd gone to infant school. Big fat tears rolled down my face while my mum was taking communion inside the church. I suddenly felt as if a ten-ton chain mail vest had been lifted off my shoulders and dumped in a pile of links and chains at the side of me. It was what I would call an 'Excalibur' moment; I was free! Free from the guilt, but also from a huge sense of failure, both personal and professional. I knew I'd let both God and myself down, and my music career had hardly been overwhelmingly successful.

In the New Year, my dad asked me to think about work of some sort. So I signed up as a trainee postman. The first day on the job, I turned up for work at six in the morning, which was strange for me as I'd been used to getting to bed at that time. I was assigned to an old postie, a nice, kind fellow with a wicked sense of humour, who showed me the ropes.

First, we had to sort the mail by hand, put the letters into the right order for the round with elastic bands wound tightly around them, and then put them in the mailbags. I was given two bags, one to drop off and hide in a hedge to pick up later, and one to use for the first part of the round. The first half wasn't so bad.

We walked all round Broomhill and part of Crookes, dropping letters off. But the second half seemed to take forever. I couldn't figure out why the bag seemed so heavy. Towards the end of my round I noticed a load of rubble in the bottom of my bag.

'Thanks lads,' I muttered, grinning ruefully.

Overall, I enjoyed the life of the postman. Sometimes you'd meet scantily clad ladies on the doorstep. Other times you'd meet an old lady who would always assure you that her dog, 'Doesn't bite, dear. You'll be all right.' But in reality, the beasts always did.

There was one little dog in Taptonville Road on my round who always went for me. It was like a rat on a stick, and it would always try and bite me. I regularly used to fantasise about wrapping a couple of laxatives in ham and feeding it to him. Now that would have sorted out Mrs Erstwhile's quality Persian carpet in one fell swoop!

After a while, I got bored of getting up early, being bitten by strange dogs and developing a funny rash on my hands from handling all the various bits of manila correspondence. So when a local singer called Mark Williamson rang up to ask me to join his band, I thought I'd have a go.

They were a great bunch of blokes who coped with this cocky misfit bass player with great tolerance. I made one album with them, and had my first ever song recorded as well. It was called 'Junior'. The opening lyric ran like this

> Too many people always pushed him around,
> Junior never found his way,
> Mum and Dad were always crying out loud,
> He was hurt but he wouldn't say,
> He'd go up in his room, cry in his pillow,
> If that was love he was sure not to follow that way

'Junior' by Nick Battle
Copyright © 2007 Star Street Music Ltd. Used by permission.

Incidentally, the band also featured a young and very talented man called Chris Eaton. He would go on to have a wonderful career as a writer penning songs for people as diverse as Janet Jackson, Amy Grant and, of course, Cliff Richard, for whom he wrote 'Saviour's Day'. I had no idea that almost fifteen years later I would be signing Chris to the music publisher Windswept Pacific Music Ltd that I worked for from 1993–99.

Around the same time I also got a call from Simon Humphrey, an old mate of mine who had been one of the in-house engineers at CBS Studios in the late seventies.

'Look,' he said, 'I've been doing some recording for Arista Records and I've got all this kit in my house. Why don't you come down and we'll cut some tracks?'

So off I went for a few days down to Nicky Graham's house, where Simon Humphrey and his production partner in their company, Steve Levine, also lived. We cut five songs with me and Simon playing all the instruments, and a fantastic drummer called Graham Broad providing the rhythm end of things. Simon and Steve arranged a couple of meetings with record companies. But nothing ever really connected.

C'est la vie.

Around this time, I fell for a girl I will call Sienna. She was the first lady to break my heart. I'd been aware of her for a few years through mutual friends and always quite fancied her. Whenever I would play Sheffield she'd turn up. But this time when I met her, something happened.

I was broken, a failed musician and going nowhere. I was probably viewed as highly dangerous by her parents. But she took me on and for a while at least, I like to believe, loved me. She was beautiful, fun, ambitious, and a former ballet dancer. An injury had forced her to give up and she was then working for the local newspaper.

I didn't have much going for me at all. But when I did become a postman, she was genuinely proud of me and demonstrably so in front of her parents. Anyway, I managed to blow the relationship over a period of almost a year, by being a neurotic, bumbling, controlling mess. She very sensibly decided to cut her losses; well, at least the first time round.

When she did, I basically cracked up. Dad told me it was my own fault for being so selfish, and he was right. But it certainly didn't help. I rang her home, and wrote to her to see if she'd change her mind, but she (and/or her parents) was implacable.

I'd take my father's car, drive for hours and then sit outside her house staring at her bedroom window, hoping for a sign of life, just a glimpse of her. I was besotted. My lost love.

I felt betrayed. Even though I would have to acknowledge that I brought a lot of what happened on myself, it was yet another aching void that had been created. My heart was like a big block of cheese riddled through with holes, as a result of personal infractions and the loss of innocence and love.

I became almost suicidal. After going to see Secret Affair (an eighties mod group) play at Leeds Town Hall, I drove home down the motorway in my dad's car. High as a kite on free cocaine (how easily we can fall back into bad habits) I aimed the car for the embankment. I chickened out at the last moment as the car's tyres squealed and I struggled to straighten the steering out.

Do you know what? It takes a lot more courage to carry on living and stare your demons down than to give up. *Much* more.

I got a job at a steelworks in Tinsley, in the industrial end of the city, working for Manpower. I was part of a rough bunch of lads whose job it was to scrub down 30-foot high lathes by hand with acid in order to clean them up ready for sale.

It was the early eighties. Margaret Thatcher and her like were busy ripping the heart out of the steel and mining industries in the north. There was a lot of unemployment, and what had been the city's foundation, Sheffield Steel, was being systematically eroded. Huge factories that had once thrived manufacturing steel for all sorts of uses, were now closing down. Countless men, and subsequently their families, lost their livelihoods. It was a bitter time.

On my first day at work, I turned up in my old stage clothes, as I didn't have much else to wear. I wore a pale blue baseball shirt, pink corduroy trousers, one white shoe and one black one. You don't need to be a rocket scientist to work out the kind of reception I received from my workmates, who were mostly ex-Army, ex-cons and a whole load of other social misfits like me.

They were great men though. They were a funny bunch too; they'd lob an aerosol can into the furnace as you walked by, to see how fast you could hit the ground. Believe me, I became good at that one. And these men worked hard. It was real physical labour. At lunchtime we'd go to the pub, deck three pints and be sober as judges, simply replacing some of the fluids we'd lost.

From time to time, and without warning, the foreman would bring his shotgun to work and set about blasting pigeons off the roof. This could be more than a little disconcerting when you were 30 foot off the ground with a bucket of acid in one hand and a wire brush in another. Suddenly you'd hear this massive bang, followed by a lump of blood and feathers flying through the air. He wasn't always a great shot.

It was a tough time in many ways. I'd lost Sienna. My career in music was going nowhere. But After the Fire were taking off. Having had a Top 40 record with 'One Rule For You', they had just released their second CBS album *80-F*. I was pretty clueless about everything.

Two blokes from the factory helped get me through. As for the rest of the lads . . . well, if ever you found yourself in a tight corner, they wouldn't suddenly disappear. They'd stand with you. One or two might even enjoy the fight. These were real men, working men, who played for keeps.

When the work was done in that particular factory, I decided to move down to London again and have another go at the music business. But it wouldn't be the last time I'd see Sienna or, indeed, dream about her.

9

IF AT FIRST YOU DON'T SUCK SEED

I'd get home at five in the morning. Waking at noon, I would find the lounge full of charismatic Christians singing to God. Half asleep and exhausted from the previous night's gig, I would wander through this meeting to take a bath.

I'd hung out for a while with some friends in Notting Hill, until I got myself sorted out. Eventually I did, and for the best part of eighteen months, I lived in a damp basement flat at Princes Square, Bayswater. Initially I shared it with an Indian bloke called Nanda and his mate from up north. Nanda and I shared a bedroom, him on the top bunk with myself on the bottom. He used to talk and shout in his sleep until one night he fell out of bed and crashed on to the floor. After that I got to sleep on the top bunk. Actually, I think Nanda and his friend found me a little strange, and over time I gradually scared them off. I didn't mean to, I just think that we had conflicting lifestyles. They were kind, though. When my former manager was tragically killed in an accident, they found a car and put some petrol in it so I could drive up the motorway for his funeral.

During this time, Sienna moved down to London and we dated briefly again before she once again kicked me into touch. Actually it felt like she kicked me in the crotch. It was one of those classic scenes. We'd celebrated New Year together. I thought we'd had a lovely, if slightly tense, time. I was scared stiff she'd dump me again. A few days later, that is exactly what she did – for the final time. As we stood in Tottenham Court Road, she told me it wasn't going to work and said 'Goodbye' as huge lumps of snow fell from the sky, and big salty tears fell down my face.

You know the phrase, 'Now is the winter of our discontent'? Well, it was.

Back in Princes Square, there was no central heating, just a one-bar fire in one of the bedrooms. It was damp and the only hot water we could get was from a small boiler over the kitchen sink. When it was bath time you had to attach a garden hose to the tiny boiler, run the hose from the kitchen through the lounge to the bathroom by the front door. By the time the bath was full, the water was tepid. In addition, bits of plaster would occasionally flake off and fall on you when a lorry went past outside. I'd enjoyed warmer times.

I found two mates – both called Pete – and they moved in. One had a prodigious appetite for the female sex. The other Pete and I were forever fielding phone calls and generally acting as his PA.

We nicknamed ourselves Bouncy, Blondie and Brainy. I was Bouncy. They were crazy, happy times. We had hardly any money; I can remember living on water and cornflakes for the best part of two weeks. I was generally kept alive by pots of taramasalata and pitta bread from my friend Rachel and, when I could afford it – a McDonald's.

Writz, the band I'd left when I lost the plot, had transformed themselves into a new unit called Famous Names, and had decided to tour like a circus act. We had kept in touch, and I found out they had a fire-eater, a dance/mime troupe called Shock and some female wrestlers.

When they played the Venue in London they also had a bear costume.

'Here you are, Ollie,' said Fairnie, using the nickname the band had given me. 'Put this on and just before the wrestlers come on, run round the gig and blow out all the candles on the tables.'

I took to my new task and role with gusto and had soon extinguished most of the candles. It was then that I set my sights on the lady wrestlers running through the crowd. I started banging on the sides of the wrestling ring. I was about to climb in, when one of the ladies concerned suggested that – how shall I put this – if I wanted a remote chance of fathering any children in the future that I should **** off out of it.

I did as I was told but not literally.

After the show I met LA, Rob Pereno, Tik and Tok, Barbie and Carole Caplin, known collectively as Shock. They were being managed by Iain Burton and Michael Summerton, who also looked after Hot Gossip. And so it came to pass that they needed a tour manager and I needed a living. If I remember rightly, I think I was paid the princely sum of £15 a day. I'd get up at eight o'clock in the morning, pick the band up, drive them to the gig, set the light show up, do the gig, pack the lights away and drive home or stay in a grotty hotel, normally getting to bed about two o'clock the next morning. I used to call them 'my little nest of vipers'. It was a term of affection . . .

Tik and Tok, who went on to have a cult following of their own, performed extraordinary robotic mime and dance pieces which were totally convincing. It was as if they could isolate every muscle in their bodies. At times they would appear almost frozen, such was their skill. Barbie, who was a real sweetheart, has found happiness with George Kajanus from the seventies pop group Sailor. Carole went on to be the Blairs' special friend, and as for the rest, sadly I can't tell you. Anyway, it was a colourful time.

It was the era when Ultravox and Visage were having such a massive impact with synthesisers and drum machines and we used to go to Blitz and Le Beatroute clubs looking every inch like a bunch of foppish dandies. I wore quite a lot of make-up, mainly rouge and eye-liner. The whole scene was glamorous and over the top.

After the punk explosion of the seventies, with the nihilism and desire to destroy everything, to be a New Romantic was to celebrate life, colour, art and fashion. It was also quite a deca-dent scene. Shock played out their role in what were, at times, highly charged erotic performances. It was a strange place for a Christian. Yet it didn't feel alien. I liked these people and, I reasoned, where would Jesus be?

Gary Numan – who had burst onto the scene with The Tubeway Army and his mega-hit 'Are Friends Electric?' – started hanging out with us. I think he may have fancied Carole, who was always a beauty. I remember after a gig one night, I think it might have been in Nottingham, he and Carole followed our little van down the motorway in his white Corvette Stingray, no doubt probably playing his big hit of the time, 'Cars'. It looked incredibly cool, but broke down a few miles into the journey home. I think that's when he might have taken up flying! I liked Gary; he was a nice bloke.

Through looking after Shock, I became friendly with John L. Walters from the group Landscape. They had pioneered the use of an electronic instrument called a Lyricon – a bit like a cross between an oboe and a synthesizer. They had a big hit record as a result with a song called 'Einstein A-Go-Go' to which Shock would also perform a live routine.

I was sold out on the whole New Romantic thing. When I could afford it, I would buy frilly shirts, and on one occasion a stunning dogtooth zoot suit designed by Jane Kahn. She let me have it at a bargain price which was kind of her.

I signed a deal with John Glover's Street Tunes records and recorded two tracks with John L. Walters producing – 'Big Boys Don't Cry' and 'On My Own Again', which I wrote with Karel Fialka. I made a video above a launderette in Southfields, London, featuring, among others, Bev from Writz and Barbie from Shock. To this day, that video makes me, my family and my friends cry with laughter (and the record went nowhere!). Imagine an earnest young man with hair and 'a waistline', plastered in make-up, doing his best to imitate Adam Ant. That sums up this particular crime against music. But perhaps even that description doesn't do it justice. So, once again, I went back to square one.

Having given up tour management to make my record, I was literally scratching around for gigs, and any work to try and make ends meet. I used to play in a wine bar in Mayfair – normally after going to Westminster Chapel on a Sunday evening. Back then, the area was renowned for those who wanted to meet a high-class hooker. The girls would be wined and dined; I'd sing my own original compositions and watch as things unfolded. On a good night I was paid £15 plus a bottle of wine and a big slab of Brie which I would take home and try and make last as long as possible. The wine usually disappeared quickly.

One day my old friend from Sheffield YMCA, Richard Morrison, rang me to ask if I wanted to play a gig in Banbury.

I said 'yes', of course. I had nothing else to do! Then I quickly rang up my mate Simon Humphrey to come and play bass with me. On the train on the way home, Simon let slip that he was contracted to a small record label called Satril Records and did I want to help him make his next album? Did I! We decided to call ourselves Sporting Life. With the exception of a few instruments, we wrote, engineered, played and produced everything ourselves.

Graham Broad once again played drums and my old mate from Writz, Jules Hardwick, contributed some stunning guitar to a couple of tracks. We got paid £50 each per track, and had to give our publishing away to Satril as well. We recorded during the day at Satril Studios, Finchley Road, and at night I wrote songs with a bloke called Sasha. It was one of the happiest and most creative times of my life. And it all began with a pair of knickers.

One day, the front doorbell rang. Standing there was a very tall, pretty brunette all the way from California called Karen. She explained that some of the washing she'd hung out upstairs had fallen off the line and floated down to our basement.

So it had. Lying in our postage stamp-sized backyard were some socks and a pair of white knickers. It was a funny way to meet. Anyway, we got talking and I told Karen what I did. She told me her husband was a singer-songwriter from Yugoslavia called Alexsander Mezek, aka Alexander John normally known as Sasha to his mates.

'You must meet him,' she said.

Sure enough, a few days later he rang the front doorbell. Sasha said he was an artist, that he also knew Sir Cliff Richard, and did I fancy maybe writing some songs with him? With an alacrity that over time I've now learnt to understand, I said, 'Yes!'

So we wrote close to thirty songs together. Whenever I went round, Karen was always very kind and would nearly always feed me something or other. Sasha would get the guitar out, we'd sit opposite each other at their dining table and we'd create.

During this time Sir Cliff recorded three songs we'd written, including 'First Date', off the *Now You See Me, Now You Don't* record and 'Front Page' off the twenty-fifth anniversary album, *Silver*. The first song he ever cut, though, was called 'Take Me to the Leader'.

The day Sir Cliff was recording the vocals at Abbey Road, I got a call from Sasha saying he had invited us to the session. But I was so flat broke I didn't even have the money for the tube fare. Quick as a flash, one of the Petes – I think it was Blondie – came up with an idea.

'Let's go to Notting Hill Gate tube and busk,' he said. 'You sing your songs and I'll do robotics like Tik and Tok.'

That's exactly what we did. Forty-five minutes later, and an earth-shattering £1.60 better off, I returned to the flat, filled the bath, using the garden hose attached to the wall-mounted hot water heater in the kitchen, leapt in, leapt out, shook it all about, found my only jacket and took the tube to Abbey Road.

Abbey Road had been the recording base of the Beatles, where Pink Floyd recorded *Dark Side of the Moon*, and where Sir Cliff was recording a song that I'd written the lyrics for. Fantastic!

It was my first visit there. That was ironic, as *Abbey Road* was the first Beatles album I ever bought. I was in awe of my surroundings. I was utterly convinced this might be my big break. I followed in the Beatles' footsteps – but kept my shoes on!

When I got there, Sir Cliff was as charming and as gracious as he has always been. We went off to the canteen where, if memory serves me correctly, he had an omelette and a stack of vitamin pills. Then we went into the studio to hear the song played back.

I was in awe, it sounded fantastic, and it was the very first song he'd recorded for the new album. I was elated. Later that day, Sir Cliff kindly dropped me and Sasha back at Princes Square in his Rolls Royce, the irony of which wasn't lost on me.

Incidentally, the song never made the record.

With the excitement generated by the Sporting Life record, Henry Hadaway, owner of Satril Records, decided that Simon Humphrey and I should become his A&R men and in-house producers (A&R means 'Artiste' and 'Repertoire' aka the bloke who's responsible for the talent and the songs). This enabled us to produce a record for my old mates Steve Fairnie and Bev Sage, now called The Techno Twins.

We recorded a version of 'Falling in Love Again', arranged by Dave Hewson, and occupied the Capital Radio hitline at No. 2 for a couple of weeks. We were narrowly beaten by Queen and David Bowie singing 'Under Pressure' and debuted in the Top 75 at No. 70 where the record stayed with an anchor for just two weeks. The Techno Twins went on to record the balance of the album, but for reasons known best to themselves I was rowed out. I'm over it now, but at the time I was less than forgiving.

One day, Henry called me into his office and played me the most awful record he had found while on holiday in Spain. I can't remember my exact words, but my reply was something to the effect that it sounded like a bucket of slop but would probably sell a million. It did. It was called 'The Birdie Song'. The Tweets, a completely fictitious group, was put together and a legend was born. The Techno Twins' manager and former head of Street Tunes, John Glover, was brought in. To cut a very long story short, they had teams of 'Tweets' appearing all over the country doing live gigs dressed up as birds. Chief Tweet was my old mate Rowles from Writz. They coined it in.

For some reason, they didn't have the right number of 'Tweets' for a *Top of the Pops* performance. Henry asked me to step into the breach. I thought for all of ten seconds. I concluded I'd never feel comfortable wearing orange tights and a fluffy yellow chicken costume. So I declined. I don't think they missed me.

Simon Humphrey and I, in the meantime, decided to make an album with journalist and poet, Steve Turner. I guess we figured that if the punk poet John Cooper Clarke could be cool and sell records, maybe Steve could, too.

We had fabulous fun creating a sonic backdrop to complement Steve's insightful poetry and played a memorable one-off gig at the Arts Centre Group in Waterloo. But we hadn't thought hard enough about how Steve would deliver it. And, bless him, live it didn't quite work. So the record never got released.

I was managed throughout this period by Jonathan Cooke, who constantly looked out for my best interests, and is one of the kindest men I know. At the end, we'd had a good time and released a few records. But nobody was going to retire on it – and I'm still waiting to see a proper accounting from the music publisher responsible for collecting the money for the songs Sir Cliff recorded. Twenty six years later!

That's show business.

10

END OF THE ROAD

We were intense young men, singing intense songs for anyone who wanted to listen. Around 1983 I met a bloke called Jeff Hammer, at the Arts Centre Group, Waterloo, who was then part of a band from Liverpool called The Teardrop Explodes. Jeff was one of the keyboard players. We hung out and chatted.

A little while later, I managed to persuade him to form a studio project together called Jump The Nile. We were essentially trying to emulate bands like Tears For Fears and Japan. We managed to get a publishing deal with ATV Music Ltd through Tim Davies and Barbara Zamoyska, who helped us release our own single through PRT.

We got some interesting reviews and a session on Capital Radio, and blagged the resources to produce our own video (more comedy gold for my family). But at the end of the day that was about it. We split up and Jeff went on to play keyboards with ABC, The Stray Cats and Kim Wilde and today creates educational music programmes.

By now I was living in the Fulham Road with two girlfriends, Annie and Sue. Sue was an air hostess, a glamorous blonde lady who I used to drive nuts. Every time she'd come home from a long haul trip and go into the kitchen to have some cereal, *somebody* had always got there first and eaten the lot . . . I was a lousy flatmate, frequently broke, and could always be relied on to empty the larder. Fortunately, both Sue and Annie were very kind and tolerant of the wastrel in their midst. Annie in particular always made sure I didn't starve and was a great pal through this time.

I can't remember going to church a lot, but I do remember Annie and Sue holding Bible studies in our flat. I used to enjoy these as I always liked a good old banter and discourse. But it also had the advantage of bringing some very godly Christian women into my life . . . very attractive, too. So this was in no way a hardship, but at times a really profound and joyous thing!

After a while, as penury beckoned, I retreated once again to my dad's in Sheffield. Apart from the very occasional radio programme for Radio Hallam, I did very little. I hung out, drank beer, got fat and became depressed.

Eventually, having had enough of this, I moved back down to London yet again. Thanks to my friend Pete 'Willie' Williams who introduced me, I moved in with a family called the Doneys in Crouch End, North London. They were – and are – lovely people. Malcolm and Meryl are both writers and their two kids, Ellie and Lewis, were easy to be around.

Through my friend Jules Hardwick, I managed to get a job three days a week as a tour guide at Highgate Cemetery, London, where Karl Marx, Charles Cruft (as in the dog show) and Bram Stoker (author of the *Dracula* novels), among many other notables, are buried.

My style at this point might have been construed as a little eccentric. I had long, curly, blond hair, a sweeping grey overcoat, a silver-topped walking cane, and on my head I sported a black beret. I must have looked like a cross between Frank Spencer and Quentin Crisp. But that is how I was portrayed in the London fashion magazine *I-D*. I might have felt I was a mover and shaker – cool and perhaps even a little aloof – but the grim reality was I was working in a cemetery. Still, it was tremendous fun. If we had a party of particularly gullible tourists we would sometimes embellish our tales a little. It would go something like this

Just over there through the glade, lies the grave of General Sir Richard Chilly Pine-Coughin [pronounced coffin], who led our troops in a particularly gallant action in the Crimean War. He was the last man standing at the Siege of Sevastopol but sadly was shot in the Dardanelles from which tragically he never fully recovered.

These flights of fancy would sound almost plausible to me, let alone the hapless tourists straining to walk around the cemetery laden with outsized cameras and rucksacks.

I stayed in touch with my pal Annie, who was a fantastic session singer and sang with Culture Club, Cliff Richard, Simple Minds and Level 42 and who, at this point, was singing with eighties' pop sensation Kajagoogoo. It was through her introduction and friendship that I came to meet the lads and their charismatic manager Paul Ryan.

I think I must have been about twenty-six or twenty-seven. I wasted no time in asking them to manage me. So it came to pass that I was managed by Kajagoogoo Ltd – the group that gave us 'Too Shy'. It was actually another low point in my life. I reverted to my rock 'n' roll bad habits and generally made an ass of myself. I suspect that deep down I knew this was my last chance as a performer and I probably wasn't going to make it.

I set about once again slowly imploding. I didn't care. Most of my mates were married. Some had kids. I was just caning it. I'd get in late at night to the Doneys' house, blitzed, and would stare in the mirror for hours, trying to find the man inside, or any sense of a soul still breathing. I didn't care if I lived or died. Apart from the occasional twinge of guilt as I indulged myself, I didn't give a toss about God, either.

When Kajagoogoo split up, Steve the guitar player and a drummer mate of his called Paul from Classix Nouveaux asked me to front a band for them. We started to write songs for what we thought would be our first album. Halfway through, I got a phone call at home in my new flat (yes I'd moved yet again), firing me from the band.

That was it. I ended up working for a building company owned by Paul the band's manager, breaking rubble and laying concrete floors. I can remember one day crying my eyes out, sat in all the muck and dust in the basement of this development. I was broken. How did I get here? I didn't have a real job, I was once again more or less completely skint, and there was no love in my life. No love for anyone. It was the end of a long road. It was the end of clinging on to a dream that was never going to happen. I wasn't Sting, I didn't have his talent or his looks; at this point for me it was 'game over'.

Time to own up.

11

YOUNG, GIFTED AND BROKE

Pot-less, car-less and clueless, I was living in Crouch End, London. It was 1986. I went round to Pete 'Willie' Williams, my pal from Sheffield (who since February 1983 had been working for U2), and he helped me draft a letter which I sent to everybody who was anybody in the music business. It went something like this

> Dear Sir,
> I am young, gifted and broke, with ten years' experience as a performer, songwriter and producer, and a great set of ears etc. etc.
>> Yours sincerely,
>> Nick Battle

You get the idea. Just three people replied. They were Clive Banks, who was then managing director of Island Records, the company founded by Chris Blackwell and to whom U2 were signed; Muff Winwood, the legendary CBS A&R man; and Jeremy Pearce, who ran Miles Copeland's and The Police's music publishing companies and who my mate Tracey Watson (who I knew from Kajagoogoo days) worked for.

Clive got me to write some lyrics for a project, but nothing came of it. Muff told me I was too old to be starting out as an A&R man at the age of twenty-eight, and Jeremy Pearce asked me to see him. Nothing happened after the first interview. But I kept dropping in to see Tracey and, when I did, I'd remind Jeremy that he needed somebody young and talented like me to go out and sign some stuff. I also said I'd work for very little money. Eventually he relented. I was hired as a talent scout for Illegal Music and Metric Music. I was given a one-page agreement which stated that I was to be paid £6,000 plus 15 per cent of the net share of the publisher's income of anything that I introduced to the company.

That means if the company earned £100,000 from something I signed, after they paid the writers' share – probably 70 per cent of that (£70,000) – I would receive 15 per cent of whatever was left, in this case £30,000. That meant I would be paid an additional £4,500. It wasn't a fortune. But for a bloke fresh off a building site with no obvious career prospects, I grabbed it with both hands. I couldn't believe my luck.

Two weeks into my new job, Miles Copeland, the owner of all the companies and manager of The Police, came back from Los Angeles. I could hear Miles and Jeremy arguing vociferously in the office next door. It would appear Miles wasn't happy at the fact that Jeremy had hired me, without also telling him that he'd given me a profit share of everything I signed. Jeremy came by later that day and tactfully suggested that I should work from home for a couple of weeks until Miles went back to America. That's just what I did. When I went back to work, Jeremy explained that my deal as it had stood would have to be torn up, but in return I would be paid a flat fee of £7,500 per annum. I accepted. After all, the last thing I wanted to do was go back to working on the building site.

Next time Miles came back from the States he still blanked me, so I took to wearing my old stage clothes to try and prompt a response from him. Finally, one day, I was wearing a yellow jacket with matching yellow shoes, and he looked at me with his flinty eyes.

'Ah, great shoes,' he said.

'Er, thanks,' I mumbled. Miles had spoken to me! From that moment I figured it was all going to be cool. And, you know, it was.

Through my pal Paul Weighell I found a band called The Christians, a bunch of brothers plus a chap called Henry Priestman from obscure seventies band The Yachts. Miles loved them, and played their music to Sting who, I believe, was potentially up for producing them. As it worked out, Sting had a movie to make – it might have been *Brimstone and Treacle* – and The Christians signed to Island. However, it put me on the map with Miles. The Christians' biggest hit was the Isley Brothers tune 'Harvest for the World', although they also teamed with PWL for a charity record, 'Ferry Across the Mersey', which also featured Holly Johnson, Paul McCartney and Gerry Marsden. But my favourite Christians' track was 'Ideal World'.

As a result I was given an airless, windowless office in the basement of 194, Kensington Park Road (just round the corner from where I used to live). I had a machine that extracted water from the air, from which I would empty at least a bucket of water on a daily basis.

Also in the basement was Martin Turner, former bass player from Wishbone Ash, who had a studio next door to my office. It was an exciting time. Through Jeremy, I had my first taste of management as well, looking after Phil Saatchi, the younger brother of Charles and Maurice (Saatchi & Saatchi) and a lovely man, who was signed to A&M Records.

We toured all over Europe with Joan Armatrading and Level 42 (my pal Annie McCaig was singing with them), spent a fortune, made one record and then got dropped. In the eighties, record companies were not gun shy when it came to budgets. One day Jeremy came in and dropped a bombshell.

'I've been asked to go and work at CBS International,' he said, 'and I've accepted.'

Back then, CBS were one of the most influential and important record labels around. They were home to Bob Dylan, Bruce Springsteen, Billy Joel and many more legendary acts. I was full of questions. I was pleased for Jeremy, because he'd been so kind to me but also apprehensive as to what would happen.

'I've suggested to Miles that he makes you head of publishing,' he added, 'on a salary of £12,000 a year.'

Jeremy had really looked after me, for which I am eternally grateful. He gave me a chance when no one else would. Incidentally, he went on to be very instrumental in signing Oasis as part of the Creation Records deal to CBS. He was a nice man and a brilliant, tenacious negotiator. I learned loads.

Not long after, my mate Karel Fialka, with whom I used to write songs, came to see me. He played me a song called 'Hey Matthew', about his son. The gist of the song was the question, 'What are you going to do when you grow up?' with Karel asking the questions and Matthew providing the answers.

'This is great, Karel,' I said, 'can you wait a couple of weeks until we've moved offices?'

In the meantime, I heard through the grapevine that Miles was looking for a general manager to look after the day-to-day running of the record company. I knew that they'd interviewed about five people for the job. So I went to see Steve Tannett, managing director of IRS Records.

'Look, why don't you just pay me some more money and I'll do that job as well?' I said.

Steve, who since Jeremy had left had kept a brotherly eye on me, went to Miles, and it was agreed. At the same time I gave them the cassette of Karel Fialkas' 'Hey Matthew'. It was to be my first signing for records and publishing and got to No. 9 in the UK charts. It was also a hit in France and Germany, selling a total of 500,000 copies.

Miles showed his thanks on the day the record debuted in the chart. He grabbed me and Steve in a simultaneous headlock – one under each arm – and ran us round and round the building.

'These guys are great,' he shouted, 'totally great!' Or words to that effect.

The times at IRS were incredibly exciting. We felt anything could happen – and it frequently did. I made some great friendships which I've kept to this day, and enjoyed a lot of laughs, too.

A couple of instances spring to mind. One of the company directors was a big, jovial, funny man, larger than life, and incredibly bright. But he wore a wig. Actually, he wore three – one for when his hair had just been cut, one for when it was a little longer, and one to show that his hair was in need of a trim. He also kept a fridge full of beer in his office.

On the day in question we'd had a long lunch, and I set about trying to renegotiate my deal. It was a hot day. The more adamant he was on any given point, the more he would shake his head, and the wig would slide forward over his brow.

Desperate to control myself, I said I had to go to the loo – where I exploded into fits of laughter. In the end, I had to leave the negotiation for another day because I simply couldn't contain my mirth any longer. I know it's cruel, but it was funny.

During this time I also got to work with The Alarm, fronted by Mike Peters. Their music was passionate and heroic and they always sold well. But they were never destined to be as big as U2, who they frequently supported, and in later years they often seemed to be on the brink of splitting up.

It was on one of these days that Steve and I went to Wales with the band to try and sort things out. As IRS was a small independent label, we always travelled cheaply. But that day was a new low. As there were no more seats on the train, we ended up in the guard's carriage with a whole load of sheep, a bicycle and loads of mail, trying to reason with the band and keep it all going.

Eventually the band split. But for a time they were great. Dave Sharp was one of the greatest rhythm guitarists of his generation, and Mike Peters was a charismatic front man. Even now when I hear one of their hits, '68 Guns', I get a shiver down my spine.

While at IRS it was my privilege to work with Colin Blunstone, a gentleman with a fabulously unique voice, who was the featured vocalist from The Alan Parsons Project. I also worked on the REM album, *Document*, which nearly got me fired. My MD, Steve Tannett, and the rest of the team were going off to a conference, leaving newly promoted 'me' in charge. Before they went, they asked if I would try an edit on the REM song, 'The End of the World'. The guys at MCA Records – who marketed and distributed us – needed a shorter version of the song for radio. This I dutifully did. However, when the band and management heard it, they went completely crazy. I remember to this day Jefferson Holt, one half of their management team back then, coming into my office and telling me *exactly* how it would be from that moment on.

They were good people though, and quite rightly very passionate about their art. Now, of course, with hindsight, I know we should never have messed with what is clearly a brilliant and epic song. But at the time I was just doing what I'd been asked to do.

One other key relationship started at IRS when I signed a young man called Kipper who made records as a band called One Nation. As an artist, he was everything I'd wanted to be. He had a soulful voice like Daryl Hall and was a cool guitar player. As proven over the last twenty years, he is an amazing talent and a wonderful friend. Kipper has produced three Sting albums, commencing with the Grammy-winning *Brand New Day*. And he is the only person in the world whose career I would ever want to manage. So I do. And it's a privilege.

Incidentally, Miles Copeland did me a massive favour when he lent me the money for a deposit on my very first home – interest free. It was a kindness I've never forgotten.

'Everybody's gotta have a home,' he said.

He was right of course. But still today, twenty years later, a great majority of the world does not, the balance of economic power and moral responsibility still lies with the West, and still we seem largely content to do the minimum possible. We're so blessed. If only we could all learn to give more away . . .

Eventually, through pressure of work, I nearly had a nervous breakdown. I became head of A&R for The Bugle Group (which was the new company name), saw a band called River City People at the Greenbelt festival and introduced them to Miles and Tony Brinsley, his associate for management. They ended up doing quite well – and I started to believe my own hype.

Still in touch with my fragile ego, at the very time when I should have stayed put, I met a man who could charm the birds from the trees. He had a knack for soliciting money from record companies that was simply breathtaking. And I believed every word he said.

'You've got talent,' he said. 'Why don't we form our own record company? You can A&R, and we'll do the radio and TV promotion.'

'He's right, I have got talent,' I said to myself.

What a fool. My life was about to turn upside down, all over again – for a whole host of different reasons.

So I resigned.

12

THE ADMIRAL'S DAUGHTER

It was Greenbelt, 1988. Having performed many times at the festival in the past, I thought I'd try and do something perhaps a bit more practical. So I decided to work in one of the charity shops as a volunteer. My faith felt steadier and I was part of a group of mates who met at the house of my former landlord and landlady, Malcolm and Meryl Doney, in Crouch End to study, read and discuss the Bible, and I wasn't abusing my body any more. But I was lonely. Having spent time with many female friends trying to find out if they were 'The One', and discovering through a series of painful adventures they definitely were not, I was now ready to find a soul mate.

So by the time I first met Lynn Bethan Bonner Edwards – introduced by my friend Adrian Reith in the Greenbelt shop – I was ready. Within minutes we were talking about her aunt and my mum both being alcoholics and how heartbreaking it was. We hung out together for most of the festival. Then she just disappeared.

My first impressions? She was one of the most engaging people I'd ever met, with a smile that could light up Oxford Street, and was possessed of immense charm. She was also, as I found out later, incredibly strong-willed, with a great sense of humour and a laugh that was free, and drew you to her. She'd just come back from a sailing holiday in Turkey and was looking gorgeous, suntanned and blonde. She spoke with passion about her faith and real sadness about her aunt. She listened carefully and was considered when she talked to me, as if she was weighing everything up. She was beautiful and yet I felt she was a wise soul. A dynamic package. I think she took my heart captive on that very day.

Four days after the festival, I tracked Lynn down and left messages for her at her office and at her home. I finally got to speak to her.

'I might be free in a couple of weeks,' she said.

I was not amused. I was used to ringing up girls and inviting them out on my terms, normally that night, or at the latest, the next one. This was not how things usually happened. Nonetheless, we agreed to meet.

'Thanks very much, see you soon,' she said after our first date. When I'd normally move in for a kiss, she got out of the car and disappeared inside her flat.

She said later she was just confident, because she knew she'd see me again. When I did see her, it was at Sport Relief and she'd brought her friend along. Not only that, but also we were going to see her sister Sian who was working for the charity. Throughout the day I did my best to keep cool, chatting politely to her friend and being as charming as possible.

'But when am I going to have her to myself?' I thought.

Finally we ended up on our own, at a wine bar in Crouch End. She asked me lots of questions. And as we left, she looked me straight in the eye.

'Are your decks clear, then?' she asked.

'Yes,' I said.

They were . . . just.

Lynn worked as an account manager for a marketing company called DCBA (we used to joke that the initials stood for 'Don't Come Back Again') based in North London. She owned her own home in West Hampstead, which she shared with her youngest sister, Sian. And outwardly at least, she appeared to be very together.

With the charming man (we'll call him Ray), I set about establishing what was to be our record label. First, we had to agree my deal. I remember the negotiation well. Ray and his partner in the record label (I'll call him Reg), were sitting in the restaurant when I arrived.

'Well, what do you want? What's the deal?' said Ray.

'I want £45,000 a year, a BMW Cabriolet and a scarlet Macaw in a brass cage six foot by four foot,' I said without cracking a smile.

'That seems OK,' said Reg.

'You can have the Macaw,' said Ray, quick as a flash.

It was a solitary moment of humour in what was to prove a disastrous enterprise. We decided to cover the classic song 'Up On the Roof', written by Gerry Goffin and Carole King and made famous by The Drifters. I approached my friend Kipper, who agreed to co-produce the record with me and Sandy McLelland (who was giving us the studio time). Then I talked to one of my pals, who was then head of promotion at one of the major labels. He fancied being a 'pop star' for five minutes, and agreed to sing and front the whole thing. I also wrote and sang the 'B' side, just to make sure if it did hit the charts that I'd make a little extra money.

It started off well enough. My friend appeared on television programmes like *Going Live*, *Wogan* and, if memory serves me correctly, *The Chart Show*. But Radio 1 only ever 'C'-listed the record, which meant we didn't receive the amount of plays we really needed, and it never took off.

But that wasn't all. Reg had not been forthcoming with the funds for all of his part of the deal. So Ray jotted down the money spent so far, and instructed me to go and ask him for his share of the costs, a sum in the region of £15,000. This I dutifully did.

When I got there, it appeared that he was – how shall I put this? Not as coherent as he might have been. He began to rant and rave. The conversation appeared to go round and round in circles. The whole process lasted a terrifying two hours during which I was shouted at, called a liar, and threatened with being beaten up. I didn't get the money. I went back to Ray's office and quit.

There was only one problem. I'd just fallen in love with the lady who was to become my first wife. And I was now unemployed.

I'd failed once again. After a short holiday with Lynn in North Wales, I met with Ray and his affable colleague, in his promotion business, who suggested I become a 'plugger' like them, so as I was broke that's what I did and then began lobbying radio and television programmes to play my artists' records, interview them, or show their video. Ray and partner

– as they were teaching me – acted as consultants at a rate of 30 per cent of everything I earned. They let me use a tiny office for a heinously high rent. I remember quite clearly that things were so parsimonious that on one occasion I was billed for tea bags and loo rolls. Well at least it wasn't itemised!

Back then all sorts of scams used to go on, to try and garner exposure for artists and records. I remember one female producer being bought a very expensive set of lingerie by one male record plugger eager to curry favour. Another producer sent word back to one record company that he might be more inclined to play a particular track if a satellite dish was installed in his home . . .

Allegedly, one former producer has retired abroad on the proceeds of their business with one promotion firm. There were always lots of tall stories flying around, and all sorts of shenanigans. Sometimes, far too many records were left with the recipients free to take them home and give them away to their mates, or flog them to their local second-hand record store. As a Christian in business, the playing field isn't always level. That's primarily because you're playing by one set of rules – what you're taught from the Bible – and the world has its own agenda. I didn't always get everything right, but you have to try.

In my work, I preferred to be creative, if at times a little naff. For example, when promoting a band called The Flame, I hired a fire engine to take the band round London dressed as firemen. We'd run up the ladder and try and throw records through windows to try and get some attention. It wasn't a hit.

My new girlfriend, though, most definitely was. Lynn was the middle of three daughters born to her mum and dad, Gen and Phil. From the start, it was apparent how highly she thought of her family and in particular her father, who'd gone into the Royal Navy as a cadet and come out forty years later as Rear Admiral J.P. Edwards CB, LVO. It was clear that she'd placed him on a pedestal, and that she loved him enormously. Lynn and her family appeared to be everything mine were not; together, happy, unified and strong. It was a heady cocktail, and the fact that she respected them all so much was pretty frightening.

I knew just how important it was to be myself when she took me to meet her mum and dad for the first time. So I deliberately didn't dress up, and just wore my jeans and denim jacket.

'Well, actually, I'm in rock 'n' roll,' was my response when Lynn's mum asked what I did.

I don't think she was massively impressed. It's not what any prospective in-law wants to hear. Lynn's dad was amused, typically gracious, calm and welcoming. He was everything and more than Lynn said he would be. Welsh, and not the tallest man in the world, he is very modest about all he has achieved, affable, with a great sense of humour that Lynn inherited, and a calm dignity coupled with a quiet and tenacious drive that could be deceptive. He loves golf, fine wine, Welsh rugby, God, good company, and his family – and is one of the most inspiring people I've ever met. No big show, just a quiet, firm presence. Resolute when he has to be, relaxed when he's not. A staunch friend. His wife, Gen, is a formidable matriarch who had made enormous sacrifices while Phil had been away at sea. She bore the lion's share of bringing up the family; fiercely loyal to Phil and the family, her ideal would be to have the entire clan all living under one roof. They made a dynamic combination. They remain devoted to each other.

I managed to get through my first day with Lynn's parents. The next time we saw them was when I offered to drive them to the Lord Mayor's Banquet. On this occasion, I dressed up as smartly as possible, even wearing a tie, something I generally only do for funerals and weddings.

Lynn and I wined and dined a great deal during our courtship, and travelled up to Sheffield to see my parents, my mum in her home and my dad in his with Verlon. Generally things progressed at breakneck speed, with a lot of fun times spent with the very sociable and naturally gregarious Phil and Gen.

That Christmas, 1988, I cajoled Lynn into letting me join her wider family at Rhiewbebbyll Ganol, near Denbigh, North Wales, home of her Uncle Elwyn and Auntie 'Nonny' Salusbury. Immediately Elwyn and Nonny made me, a complete stranger, feel at home. I became fond of them both. When Elwyn passed away from leukaemia in 1995, it was my privilege to carry him and gently lay his earthly body into the ground. He was a single-minded, kind, individual man and I liked him immensely.

At this point I should explain that I used to collect parrots. I know it's mad. But some people smoke themselves stupid, others stuff their faces with chocolate and junk food, and others lose themselves in chemicals of one form or another. My new vice was birds. At one time my collection comprised

1 Scarlet Macaw called Good King Jack;
1 Salmin Amazon called Max;
1 Senegal parrot called Sam;
2 Cockatiels called Ollie and Fairnie;
1 Blue fronted Amazon called Joe.

I had been keeping Good King Jack in the office I rented from Ray in West London. But there were three reasons why he was now at home with me – he'd taken a dislike to one of the lads in the office and had started to growl at him every time he went by; somebody had also taught him the word 'bollocks' which he would use at the most inopportune moments; and when I used to leave the office he would cry like 10,000 babies all being pushed over a cliff at the same time . . . and it was getting on everybody's nerves.

It was apparent when Phil and Gen came to inspect my flat that there simply was not enough room for Lynn and all my birds. So we kept just two – Joe and Max. One Saturday before we left to go to Oxford to see Phil and Gen, I found Lynn giving Max a cup of tea.

'I'm not sure that's a very good idea,' I said. 'He's a parrot and is only used to water and his bird food. The tannin in the tea might make him ill.'

That weekend, after going to church with Lynn and her mum and dad at St Peter's in Wooton, and taking communion, I went for a walk with Lynn on the Old Golf Course in Boar's Hill and proposed to her. On returning to her parents' house, I officially asked Phil for her hand in marriage.

'Yes,' he said, amid lots of tears and hugs. 'But if you hurt her, I'll clonk you!' A sentiment I understand much more now I have two daughters.

So we were officially engaged. We drank champagne and then later, round about half past midnight, I dropped my new fiancé back at her flat in West Hampstead, before driving down to Radio 1 and leaving a record for my pal Simon Mayo who was then hosting the flagship *Breakfast Show*. The song was 'True Love Never Fails' by Jonathan Butler and Vanessa Bell Armstrong. With the record was a note from me to Simon, telling him all about the proposal and just how 'True love never fails'.

'Get out of that one, mate,' I wrote at the bottom of my note.

I went home to find Max very poorly. I made my parrot as comfortable as possible and crashed out around 2 a.m. The next thing I knew, it was 7.30. My pal Nick Fleming was on the phone telling me to put Radio 1 on. Sure enough, Simon Mayo was playing 'True Love Never Fails' as his 'Record Of The Week'.

I was elated. I was engaged to Lynn, I had the Record Of The Week on Radio 1, and life was great. That is, until I looked over at little Max, who was lying stiff as a board, in the bottom of his cage. Yes, little Max was no more.

He was . . . erm . . . a deceased parrot.

I was upset. But in my grief, I managed to relay to Simon Mayo just what had happened. Now, Simon is a very lovely man, but he does have a wicked sense of humour. So imagine Lynn's surprise when she arrived at work the following Friday.

'How could you do that,' said her PA, 'and murder such an innocent creature?'

Simon had told the entire nation about the sorry tale of Max and the fatal dose of tea that had been administered by my new fiancé. Thankfully, Lynn saw the funny side, even if Max now no longer could.

So now I was a record promoter. My job was to lobby producers and DJs to play the records I was carrying, in as many available slots as possible, and hopefully secure a place on the coveted Radio 1 playlist. Ray and his promotion partner gave me their network and unprecedented access to their media contacts – and a great if expensive start in the world of record promotion.

I decided I needed an event to boost business. I hired a boat and took Simon Mayo, Phil Schofield, the entire team from BBC1's *Going Live*, Simon Fuller and his client Paul Hardcastle and *Top Of The Pops* producer Paul Ciani down the Thames for the afternoon. We had mock award ceremonies, my pal Fairnie took the photographs, far too much wine was consumed and the sun shone. Life was very good indeed.

A couple of weeks before Lynn and I were due to get married, I drove up to Sheffield on my own, as Dad had been undergoing some tests. Typically he'd played down the whole thing. But when he'd rung, I knew it might be serious. On the way, I prayed that whatever happened, I'd be able to respond in the right way. But nothing had prepared me for what he had to say.

'I've got a form of leukaemia,' he told me. 'It's called idiopathic red cell aplasia.'

He'd done his homework and reckoned on having just three years to live. I couldn't quite take it in. When I left later that day to drive down to Oxford to see Lynn and her parents, I wept most of the way. Was my dad ever going to see any children we might have? How long exactly did he have? Would he be OK on the wedding day?

The night before the wedding, having bid my future wife goodnight, I checked into The Foxhouse Hotel with my dad and Verlon, Simon and Hilary Mayo, my best man Fairnie and of course Bev, and my dear friends Adrian and Judy Reith, not forgetting Trevor (my mate whose sofa I'd slept on when I was homeless), one of my ushers.

It was also Dad and Verlon's wedding anniversary. So I decided we would have a cake and champagne. After all, I thought, how many more would Dad be able to enjoy? A fabulous evening was had, particularly as I'd managed to get the pass key to all my mates' rooms! Loo seats were cling-filmed and toothpaste was put in the unlikeliest places. I thought I'd done well until I got back in the early hours, to find an entire black forest gateau stuck to the door handle of my bedroom.

I rose early, got on the hotel's exercise bicycle, did a few miles, and then sat in my own private Jacuzzi reading a book on the Vietnam War. It proved to be inadequate preparation for what was to come. The wedding went well, although Lynn was late(!). We celebrated in a massive marquee in my newly acquired in-laws' back garden. 'Best Man' Fairnie was the consummate entertainer, performing magic tricks.

'We could talk about scandal,' said Fairnie, 'and Nick's life could keep the entire staff of the *News of the World* busy for at least a year. But let's not go into that now.'

Phil's speech was typically moving. He was obviously incredibly proud of his middle daughter. He said some lovely things – and in particular paid credit to his wife for shouldering the lion's share of their upbringing. Afterwards, people fell in the pool although some did choose to swim voluntarily. We left as soon as we reasonably could in a gold Rolls Royce somebody had kindly lent us.

We honeymooned in the Dordogne in France for the best part of three weeks, and then came home to my flat in Nelson Road, Crouch End. When we arrived we found that Phil and Gen had spring-cleaned the entire place and left a bottle of champagne in the fridge.

I worked hard. But my education with Ray in the business of record promotion was proving too costly, and I had massive overheads. So after talking to my dad, I decided to go it alone without them as my consultants and take on a smaller office. I moved into Harley House, Marylebone Road, with my old After the Fire manager, Jonathan Cooke. It wasn't so much an office as a bit off the hall, just outside the kitchen, where I managed to squeeze in a desk and hook up a phone. I paid £25 a week for it.

'He'll be bust by Christmas,' I heard someone say.

However, I was determined to prove him wrong and continue to bring home the bacon for my new wife and my new life. I called out to God and asked him for help. After all, I reasoned, he had seen me through this far, and my experience was that if anybody ever let anybody down, it was normally me.

I felt trapped in the money pit and I was drowning not waving. Lynn was wonderfully stoic and supportive through this time. The fact that she was also earning was a godsend. Somehow my business survived. My good friend Nick

Fleming, with whom I'd had my first hit record, recommended me to people, despite the fact he wasn't making any money from it, and we started to turn a corner.

I was still to have my first hit record on my own as a promoter though, and it came from the unlikeliest of places – Australia. Well, via Australia, actually. The record was a remix of the classic fifties hit, 'She Taught Me to Yodel' by Frank Ifield. This mix featured The Backroom Boys. As Frank was in Australia and the Backroom Boys weren't interested in doing any promotion, I invented two characters – Blind 'Lemon' Hardy and William 'Dogface' Hardy – and off I went to plug the record.

I decided that Blind 'Lemon' Hardy needed a very broad Yorkshire accent, and should be dressed like a lumberjack with sunglasses on. Don't ask why, it's just what I felt like doing that day. So off I went, in my wonderful disguise, to do a bunch of interviews. First up was Neil (Dr) Fox at Capital Radio. Mike Leonard, who worked with me, played the straight man as the record promoter and introduced me to Neil as Blind 'Lemon' Hardy. I went straight into character.

"Ello, Neil, lovely to meet you. Please call me Lemon,' I said in my thick Yorkshire accent, with a perfectly straight face. 'Now then, Neil,' I went on, 'can yer get Capital in Sheffield? Are you one of them syndicated shows? 'Cos me mam would love to hear me on t'radio.'

Mike, bless him, was barely holding it together. Somehow, though, I scraped through the interview, with my disguise intact. As far as I'm aware, to this day Dr Fox is none the wiser. Actually if I'm really honest, he probably doesn't even remember it! It's just one of thousands of interviews he's done over the years.

On the Sunday, Lynn and I were with her younger sister Sian and boyfriend (now husband), Sarsfield. We were listening to the Top 40 when on it came in the chart at No. 40. The record gave me my first hit, having just scraped into the charts for one week. But my antics had not gone unnoticed by the record business and I began to get more work. Lynn used to say, 'Just keep going, babe, it will be all right,' whenever I got downhearted or worried about business.

By this time we'd managed to sell my flat in Crouch End and were now living at Lynn's old home in West Hampstead. We decided it was time to try for a baby. Four months later, Lynn became pregnant with our first daughter.

Misha Nicole Bonner Battle was born on 11 May 1992 at the Royal Free, Hampstead. I fell in love all over again. What a beautiful child. It's funny, she is now fifteen and I can still see the same expressions on her face as when she was first born, particularly when she frowns.

I wasn't a very good dad at first, although I did my fair share of nappies. I think perhaps, like a lot of males, I found that children become interesting when they really start to engage. From the point where Misha first smiled at me, though, I was smitten.

We were also blessed with two hit records – The Future Sound Of London whose record 'Papua New Guinea' debuted on the chart at No. 22 and Capercaillie's 'A Prince Among Islands', which entered at No. 39. It was as if God was saying, 'Look, here's your babe, and here's the provision. Don't worry about the future, it will be all right.'

And it was, for a while. In fact, over a five-year period we had a run of great fun work and hits which included George Benson, Cliff Richard, Ronnie Wood, David Essex (my wife loved sitting next to him at dinner), Clannad, the rock band Thunder, and we also had a hand in Take That's RCA debut, 'Promises'. We were quite often called in to help when a label needed a few extra plays on a record, and this was the case here. RCA's in-house team led by Nick Godwyn, had done a fantastic job on the band. But Radio 1 was being a little slow on the uptake. Working closely with Nick, we managed to secure a couple of extra plays and the record went in the chart at No. 38.

Anyway, back to Misha. I was a real pain and treated her like she was a piece of porcelain at first. Not having had a child before, I was frightened she could break in two at any moment. I quickly got over that, though, when I changed her first nappy. I thought about omitting that. But I suspect if Misha has read this far, there will be enough embarrassing stuff already. So I won't!

Sorry, eldest daughter!

13

I NEVER CAN SAY GOODBYE

We were in Oxford when I suddenly got the urge to see my best man Steve Fairnie who was celebrating his birthday. I talked to Lynn about it. She thought it would be a great idea if I went down to Bristol to surprise him, while she stayed with Misha and her mum and dad.

So off I trundled and got to the diner where Fairnie was enjoying his party. I remember Bev dressed up as Marilyn Monroe singing 'Happy Birthday Mr President' to him. Rowles, his long-time friend and erstwhile songwriting partner, was also there. It was a lovely time with my 'best man' and best friend.

Just two days later I got the news that he had died of an asthma attack while looking after a bunch of art students on a trip to Torbay.

Fairnie dead.

Thank God I'd been 'nudged' to go and see him. I feel it was divine intervention that I got to go and celebrate my best friend's last birthday the day before he died. It seemed impossible. The life and soul of the party, Steve Fairnie – one of the most creative and vibrant life forces on this planet – had been taken from us. How cruel for Bev, Famie and Jake. What a massive loss.

Simon Mayo paid tribute to Fairnie on his Radio 1 *Breakfast Show*. Martin Wroe wrote an obituary for *The Independent* newspaper. Bono attended the funeral along with hundreds. Fairnie's death came hard on the heels of Jules, our guitar player from Writz, losing his beloved wife Buzzy as a result of an epileptic fit on the night Bill Clinton was officially sworn in as US president.

Everybody felt clattered by it all. Poor Jules and daughter Hemmie, and now just a few weeks later poor Bev, Famie and Jake. It just didn't seem right. It wasn't right. Not in earthly terms. Where was God in all of this? I didn't know.

Fairnie's funeral was colourful, funny and joyous while at the same time being totally heartbreaking. It was a privilege to be there and has remained a privilege to continue to love his family, something which I really treasure.

A few months later, fed up with London life, not being able to park our car within a few hundred yards of where we lived, and with no real sense of community, we decided to sell up. My business had taken a downturn as Fairnie's death had impacted me greatly. Frankly, I was wallowing in my own grief a bit so we went to live with Phil and Gen in Oxford while we looked for a new home.

By now I'd left my office in Marylebone Road and was in the process of going back to my first love, songs and songwriters. I met for lunch with an old pal, Bob Grace, who informed me that he'd just been made managing director of a brand new music publishing company funded by the Japanese called Windswept.

'Do you know anybody who could be the A&R creative guy?' he asked.

'It's me,' I said, never having been backward in coming forward. The deal was more or less written on the back of a napkin, and so I was hired as a consultant.

I was commuting on the coach from Oxford on a daily basis, leaving the house at 7.30 a.m. and getting back to Lynn and my in-laws about 8.30/9ish most evenings. It was a long and tiring process. In the meantime Lynn and Verlon were scouring the towns and villages west of London for somewhere for us to live. One morning – at four o'clock to be precise – Lynn woke me up.

'I'm pregnant,' she said.

'What?' I said as I fell out of bed.

'I'm pregnant!'

'Fantastic!' I cried. And immediately felt the weight of more responsibility on my shoulders. 'How am I going to be able to sustain everyone?' I thought. But what I actually said was something else.

'Shall we tell your parents or keep quiet as it's very early days?'

'It will be hard not to tell them, living under the same roof,' she said.

'Yeah, you're right.'

So a few hours later, Phil and Gen got a little bit extra for breakfast. Needless to say, they were thrilled at the prospect of another grandchild. Of course, the pregnancy brought everything into focus, as we would now need our own space all sorted as soon as possible.

It was Verlon who found us our first home in Chorleywood. It was a lovely bungalow with three bedrooms, owned by a couple who went to the local Anglican church, St Andrew's. We loved it and bought 26, Furze View which we named *Ty Cariad*, which roughly translated from the Welsh means the 'House Of Love' or 'The Love Shack'.

We set about decorating before we moved in, with everyone – but especially Verlon – lending a hand. I would get on the coach from Oxford, go to the Windswept office in Notting Hill, do a full day's work and then take the tube out to Chorleywood, decorate for a couple of hours and then go back to Oxford to sleep.

We moved in and life was happy, if challenging financially. Lynn was now a marketing consultant to British Telecom and was travelling in and out of London a couple of days a week. I was in the throes of putting the affairs of my promotions company to bed, and trying to persuade my boss Bob to take me on full-time.

We delighted in our new home, our beautiful daughter Misha, who was nineteen months old, and our new church family at St Andrew's. Even though we didn't have much money, by and large we were very happy.

Then one day on her way in to work, Lynn nearly passed out on the tube. At first we thought it was the pregnancy, and maybe she was a little anaemic. But that was not the case. I remember the day quite clearly. Not satisfied with what was going on with Lynn, the doctor referred her to the hospital at High Wycombe.

I was at work in London when Lynn rang.

'I've got cancer!' she sobbed down the phone.

'I'm coming home now! Don't worry, I love you,' I said.

I felt sick. Fear ran through my body like a massive electric current. I started to sweat. My hands felt clammy. Waves of panic rose inside my body. I ran out of the office and drove like a madman down the A40 to Chorleywood. I was in a complete mess, my mind and heart racing at a million miles an hour. I remember very little about the journey. I was struggling to cope with it all. I was so frightened, I couldn't think clearly. I was sobbing and raging at God, all at the same time.

'Why? Why? Why? Why Lynn, why me, why us? *Why?*'

The next few days, weeks and months were to be a living hell. I would experience what it was like to feel really deep, excruciating, emotional pain. But what about my lovely wife? What would she have to go through? Unknown to us both, we were embarking on a journey that would have disastrous consequences for us all.

We would have to try – as Bruce Cockburn wrote – to 'kick at the darkness till it bleeds daylight'. Would we have the strength do to so? Only God knew.

14

THE 'C' WORD

We entered into a never-ending round of meetings with the medical profession. Lynn had a lump in her breast which they said was malignant. They advocated a complete mastectomy (removal of the entire breast) followed by a caesarean section six weeks later to bring the baby prematurely into this world so that she could commence chemotherapy and finally radiotherapy.

Dr Roger Vass the consultant was professional, kind and firm, and advocated that we throw everything at the cancer to try and stop it in its tracks. I looked at Lynn, then looked him straight in the eye.

'If it was your wife sat here,' I said, 'would you be advocating the same procedure?'

'Yes,' he said quietly.

We reluctantly took his advice.

I remember the morning of 3 December 1993 very clearly. The night before, I'd stayed with Lynn for as long as I could. But that morning as she was having an operation that would hopefully save her life, I was wandering around her parents' home in Oxford, crying out to God for help and feeling totally powerless. I stuck my head round the door to the little sitting room, and saw Phil holding my baby daughter Misha with big, silent tears rolling down his face. Poor Phil, poor Gen. What a nightmare for any parent.

Nothing can prepare you for cancer, particularly when you're young. There are no courses that anyone wants to volunteer for. Here we were, married for just three years with one child, and Lynn pregnant with our second, facing a radical

75

mastectomy, chemotherapy and radiotherapy. The only thing you can do is ask as many questions as you can, and do not leave your doctor until you are completely satisfied with the answers they have given you. Note I said satisfied – not happy.

One other thing Dr Vass mentioned was that Lynn would have her ovaries removed as the cancer was oestrogen receptive. Breast cancer is a nightmare that involves an aggressive attack on a woman's fundamental femininity and sexuality. The loss of a breast is bound up with how a woman feels about feeding her child, feeling sexy, feeling whole. For the man, too, it is a nightmare to see his beautiful wife at the end of a surgeon's knife, to realise that in order to save her life and/or buy her time that such rapacious ugliness has to occur. When it happens it is so profoundly shocking.

There she was, the woman I loved: her skin was grey and her eyes pinned so far back in her head from the drugs, she looked like she was never going to land.

'They've taken it away,' she said, and then she started weeping, gentle, soft, sad, tired tears.

She was covered in bandages with tubes, IV lines and drains, seemingly sprouting from everywhere on her body. Choked beyond words, I held her hand. Why are we men so rubbish at this stuff? I told Lynn I loved her. The words sounded pithy under the circumstances. But we were together and we were not alone; our baby was still safe and sound inside Lynn's stomach and had survived the operation. Thank God!

Lynn drifted in and out of consciousness. Later, when she was safely asleep, I went home. One of the first calls was from her surgeon, a wonderfully sensitive man, to tell me that he felt the operation had gone well. I remember saying to him that he had a very difficult job, but he did it very well and with great compassion. I then made and received thirty-odd calls before drinking way too much gin and going to bed. The last call of the day would always be to my dad. Having survived leukaemia, and quietly come to faith himself, he was praying for another miracle for Lynn.

And then it was just 6 a.m. and the phone was ringing . . . It was the staff nurse from Lynn's ward at High Wycombe hospital. Lynn was crying and wanted me there *now*. I fell into my clothes, jumped into the car and got there as quick as I could. Somebody kindly shoved a cup of coffee in my direction.

When horrible stuff happens, all you want is someone you love with you. When you fall off a bike as a kid, you want to be patched up and held, kissed and told everything will be all right. That feeling never goes away. I'm a middle-aged man, yet still there are times I want to cry and be held. Lynn simply wanted the same thing. Throughout the day her mum and dad came. It was awful for them, but they are two incredibly strong stoic people. They were brilliant with her.

Barry Kissell, one of the leaders from St Andrew's, came and prayed with us. A steady flow of medical people came and went; we were told that the cancer had spread to only one lymph node. That was good news as the lymph glands help the body's immune system to fight infection.

If you ever have to watch your partner suffer, and you're going through your own pain, try not to underestimate what their parents will be feeling. Here, Lynn was their little girl. She may have been living with me. She may have been thirty-five years old, but she was *their daughter*. Handle with care. But equally, I would advise anyone going through the same kind of thing as I did: don't let anyone swamp you. Your job is to look after your poorly partner and children first. Everybody else should do their best to get in line and support that initiative.

It was Christmas 1993, and Lynn, Misha and I were singing carols round the crib one night. My heart was silently breaking. There was my lovely wife minus a breast, fighting cancer with another unborn child inside her waiting to be big enough to be safely and prematurely delivered. We were singing 'Away in a Manger'. It was probably the first Christmas Misha would ever remember. I would have felt less pain if somebody had cut my heart out with a blunt spoon.

We had tremendous help from the family and also from St Andrew's Church. Sometimes strangers would turn up on the doorstep with ready-cooked meals.

You know, however hard-hearted one can sometimes be about the church and its cumbersome baggage (created by humans, *not* by God), when you receive an extravagant outpouring of practical Christian love – the like that we as a family have seen – it is breathtaking. It is amazing how many years of prejudice and fear can be assuaged by a simple act of love.

We saw in the New Year with Adrian and Judy Reith. Judy was also pregnant with their second child, Tilly. So at midnight, she and Lynn gently but sedately jumped off some cushions to welcome the New Year.

15

MAGIC AND LOSS

I got scrubbed up and put on a medic's gown. It was 4 January 1994, and we had gone to High Wycombe Hospital once again. I was preparing for the imminent arrival of our baby, and the equally imminent removal of Lynn's ovaries. The experience was a mixture of magic and loss.

Lynn was given a pre-med to relax her, then another drug to numb her body from the neck down. My job was to check she couldn't feel a thing by tickling her toes, etc. A tiny towel was placed over a bar so Lynn couldn't see anything, and the operation began. A few minutes later, the surgeon pierced the amniotic sac and lifted a baby girl out of Lynn's womb and on to her breast.

Welcome to the world, Jodie Nadine Boon Battle. What a miracle! The entire operating theatre cheered.

'Well done, team. Thank you!' I said.

I felt elated, delighted that Jodie was safe, and concerned she would be OK. But I felt devastated that my wife was about to lose her ovaries – and with it the ability to have more children. She would also have to face the immediate onset of the menopause.

I cried when both our daughters were born. As I remember all of this, I'm crying now, but they are tears of joy. Yes, I've had heartbreak – but I have known, and continue to know, what it is to be really loved, and to really love back.

The surgeon continued with the operation. Minutes later, Jodie, our gorgeous gift from God, was whisked off to the Special Care Baby Unit. Lynn was taken into the recovery room while I was scrubbing down, and holding one of the surgical team who was crying all over me. He'd been there for her first operation as well.

I went into the recovery room, and spoke to Lynn who wanted me to be with our daughter, Misha's new sister. There she was in SCBU, a tiny little thing under a heat lamp. Sister Mac, the nurse in charge, took a couple of Polaroids for Lynn while Jodie's entire hand enveloped my little finger. She was so lovely, so frail, so perfect.

'Please God, let her live,' I prayed. I asked for God's blessing on her life, just as we had done when Misha was born.

Over the next few weeks while Lynn tried to recover, Jodie was fed via a tube that went up her nose and into her stomach. In time Lynn was also able to feed Jodie through her one good breast, at least until the chemotherapy started – something that she really wanted to do.

A few short weeks into Jodie's life, she got a chest infection. Gen was the first to spot it, and Jodie and Lynn were rushed back into hospital. I seriously thought I was going to lose not only my wife but also my daughter; this is something I have never told anybody before. I cannot begin to articulate that. Somehow, through the phenomenal care and commitment shown by the staff at the unit, Jodie got better. Shortly after, Lynn began her first chemotherapy treatment. It was to be a desolate time.

The chemo suite. It was like walking into a grey IKEA. There was a fish tank teeming with life. Funnily enough, that was an encouraging sign; a community in action going about its normal business. Around me, there were also a lot of people going through various stages of treatment. This in itself was quite shocking.

'Some of these people may die,' I whispered to Lynn, 'but you're not going to.'

There was quite a while to wait, as first you have to have your blood test, and then your own individual, lethal cocktail is mixed up and sent to the chemo suite. There is only a limited amount of time the drug can be administered, as some of them go off very quickly. Finally, Lynn's turn came.

They placed what looked like a huge tea cosy on her head packed with ice. This is because the drug that was being administered was so strong, it could make the patient's hair fall out. Indeed, as I looked around I could see various people in stages of hair loss or thinning. To a man whose hair on a good day resembles a bald-headed eagle it would not have been a problem. But to a stunning woman like Lynn, it could be yet another aggressive attack on her sexuality.

A huge syringe was produced. It was about the size and thickness of a cucumber. Slowly and very carefully, the cytotoxic drugs were injected into Lynn's arm. I watched and wondered what effect this concoction would have on my wife's health. She was just incredible. In fact, she remains the bravest person I've ever known. She had such enormous, psychological strength.

I found visiting the chemo suite one of the most harrowing episodes of the cancer journey. In future, Lynn's loving mum Gen took her for most of the treatments. To be honest, I was pretty useless at it. I think it was the knowledge that some of the people were dying and yet some would survive. And who makes that choice? And who can live with that possibility? And why did my dear wife have to go through this? To be pumped full of lethal drugs . . . nothing made any sense just then. I'd managed, by God's grace, to cope with the operations. But somehow this was more devious, more insidious.

Over the six months Lynn took as much as she could of the treatment. Her hair thinned a little, but not so that you'd really notice. If anything, it was a little bit curlier than usual. She did get very weak for a while. Who wouldn't?

In our bathroom we had our own private pharmacy of pills and medicines to help all kinds of bodily functions, acupressure bands to counteract nausea, Chinese medicine, reflexology . . . we tried everything and more.

Lynn's family, Phil, Gen, and sisters and husbands Sue and Nat, Sian and Sarsfield, and my dad and Verlon rallied around. They were great. Consistent. Practical. Loving. Present.

Throughout all this time, I called out to God regularly – always daily, sometimes hourly. Sometimes I think he would answer my request and, at others, for reasons best known only to him he would choose not to. How did I hold onto my faith at this time? The truthful answer is, it was very difficult, as you will see later on from the journal entries I've included in the book. However, it is my belief that my heavenly Father God never once let go of my hand, but walked through the fire with me, so I was never completely alone. At times it all got a bit overwhelming, and so did I, but that's OK. Everybody had their own painful road to travel.

From the moment of diagnosis, we made the decision to throw absolutely everything at the cancer to stop it. It took great physical and emotional strength, but it was to buy us a considerable chunk of time – time for Lynn to watch her babies grow.

Straight after the chemo came the radiotherapy, and all the time Misha and Jodie, both still in nappies, were growing and developing. Radiotherapy is a very exact science. Using computer technology, the radiographer lines up exactly where they will blast you and a tiny little tattoo is put in place on your body. When you go for successive treatments they know where to pinpoint everything precisely.

My dear wife had six weeks of this. Towards the end it got more debilitating as she became increasingly tired from the accumulation of all the treatments. Finally, we got through to the end of July in 1994, with all treatments finished.

Lynn would have to take a drug called tamoxifen for at least the next five years. But that was it. Jodie was just over six months old and flourishing. Misha had turned two, and we were about to return to normality. Or were we?

My boss, Bob Grace, was incredible, and had showed real compassion in the face of it all. In return, I worked as hard as I could, when I could. I signed my old mate from the Mark Williamson Band, Chris Eaton, to Windswept. I also managed to secure recordings of his songs with Patti Austin and Michael Ball, and procure a record deal with EMI's Contemporary Christian Music division in Nashville.

I was also plugging songs to my mates at the record companies. We came up trumps when Simon Cowell recorded one of the classics from our catalogue, 'The Sun Ain't Gonna Shine Anymore' with Robson and Jerome. The album went on to sell 2.3 million units in 1995 in the UK alone.

I'd first met Simon in the early nineties when he released a 'megamix' cover version of Kylie Minogue hits produced by

Nigel Wright. It came out as *The UK Mixmasters*. I seem to remember it stuck at No. 43 because radio didn't like the way the record had been cut together.

Simon was an amazing promotions person even then, particularly when it came to TV. Every single time I would ring up a key telly programme, I always found that he'd beaten me to it. He is, and remains, one of the best record men in the world. Although, back then, we were both still trying to perfect our game.

I signed some fabulous songwriters to Windswept. They included Steve Booker, who had songs recorded by Natalie Imbruglia, Boyzone, Paul Young and Martina McBride to name a few. Julian Gallagher, son of Benny from Gallagher and Lyle, was another signing we had success with, most notably again with Simon Cowell and his group Five and the song 'Got The Feelin'' which sold 250,000 singles in the UK alone. It was a cracking little record.

And then came the Spice Girls. They were magic all right.

16

SPICE UP YOUR LIFE

We had some modest success. The company was growing steadily. Through the end of 1994–95 I continued to work for Windswept, and became general manager of the company. I'd brought my friend Ivan Chandler in as film and TV consultant. He put together an excellent documentary with Christmas Films and BBC2 on the legendary songwriter Burt Bacharach, who we represented.

One day, Ivan came into my office and told me about a new girl group Simon Fuller was putting together. I knew Simon from my days as a record promoter, and had a great respect for him. He is bold, innovative, and a great strategist when it comes to artists' careers. He had guided Paul Hardcastle to No. 1 in the USA with his song '19', and enjoyed success with D-Mob and taken Cathy Dennis to stellar heights. He was now managing Annie Lennox. So I figured with all this going on, and more, we should definitely check these girls out. Ivan kindly solicited the cassette tape for me. It was full of great songs.

I took the tape into my boss Bob and we arranged for Simon and the girls to come in. At this stage, the girls did not have a record deal, although we were aware that two record labels were interested in them, London Records and Virgin.

Our office was in a quiet cul-de-sac in Holland Park, just a few doors down from where Elton John has his town house. The girls arrived, spilling out of Geri's tiny little blue car, I think it was something like a Fiat Panda. They came bursting into the building with this amazing energy. It was like a river had just burst its banks. This torrent of noise, sassiness and laughter flooded our office. Geri and Mel B seemed to be the ringleaders and the loudest, and their energy and humour were infectious.

They poured into our boardroom. When Simon arrived a little while later in his chauffeur-driven Jaguar, they put their DAT (digital audio tape) on and danced and sang around our boardroom table, doing their routine.

My initial take on the whole situation was that I knew about the interest from the two record labels. The girls were incredibly confident, the songs brilliant, and Simon's track record spoke for itself. For Bob and me, it seemed like a complete slam dunk. But we knew everybody would be clamouring to sign them and how on earth were we going to afford it? We'd already spent our entire £150,000 budget for new talent. How were we going to make this deal work? We were just a tiny independent publisher.

The answer lay in the east with our Japanese boss, Ichi Asatsuma and the corporation Fujipacific who held the purse strings to our humble operation. Ichi flew in from Tokyo. Having taken the time to familiarise himself with their songs, he met them and agreed to come up with the necessary funds to sign them. So now we had the approval. But the race was far from won. EMI, BMG and all the major music publishing houses wanted to sign them.

In the end, thanks to the balls of Bob Grace and the support from our US and Japanese offices, Windswept won the Spice Girls.

When 'Wannabe' first came out, we thought it would do well. I even predicted in the insiders' industry paper *The Tipsheet* that it would go to No. 1. What I could never have imagined was that it would go to No. 1 in thirty-one countries. Bob and I had prayed for success and had asked God to bless our business. But we'd never imagined it would be on a scale like this.

Let me explain what a music publisher does. In this instance, we acted like a bank in advancing the girls money against future royalties, be they performance (when a song is played on the radio, television, in concert etc.) or mechanical (i.e. the royalty that is paid to the writers when a CD is sold or song downloaded).

A music publisher should also be constantly looking out for new opportunities for his writers – to get the songs recorded by somebody else or used in a commercial or in a film. If the girls had flunked out, we would have lost a substantial sum, and probably our jobs. As it was, they went on to sell well in excess of 40 million records.

So I'd been through the mire family-wise. But work was definitely on the up. And somehow, thanks to the kindness of colleagues and friends, I was still able to achieve. I realise I wouldn't be enjoying this moment quite so much if we hadn't signed the Spice Girls.

Windswept continued to grow. As a result of the Spice Girls, we were attracting shed-loads of new business. We bought old song catalogues, and got new songs recorded by artists like Natalie Imbruglia, Joe Cocker and Boyzone for our songwriters, and also signed new pop acts like the boy band 911 which Pete, our creative manager, had brought in.

Life was good. I was earning over £100,000 a year. We'd moved into what I would call a 'grown-up house' with some woodland. I had the 4x4 and the expense account. Lynn and the kids were all doing great. What could possibly go wrong?

'Now I'm feeling better,' said Lynn, 'I'd like a reconstruction of my breast.'

I'll be honest. I really didn't want her to have it done. After all we'd been through, it just felt like more gunk and pain we would all have to experience again, and no one more so than Lynn.

'I love you as you are,' I reasoned, 'I don't need you to have this done.'

But she was adamant. And who was I to deny her the opportunity to try and feel whole again? So the operation went ahead.

It was more complex and arguably more physically painful than her mastectomy. They ended up taking part of her stomach wall and using that to create the shape of a breast. Then they inserted something like a plastic-fence-come-webbing where her stomach wall had been, to give her more support down there. It was a massive operation, much bigger than the mastectomy. When I met her on the way back from the operating

Me, aged one, with my mum in the background.

With my mum toddling in the winter snow.

Nana and Wilfred on their wedding day.

Sixth form antics at King Edward VII School, Sheffield.

With Ishmael at Greenbelt.

After The Fire headlining Greenbelt in 1977.

Writz press shot. *Photo: Paddy Eckersley by kind permission of Onward Music Ltd./Cube Records Ltd.*

Yes, once upon a time I had hair! *Photo: Paddy Eckersley by kind permission of Onward Music Ltd./Cube Records Ltd.*

Playing bass with Writz.

Sir Cliff Richard, Alexander John – and me.

Desperately seeking stardom.
Photo: Paul Cox

Lynn and me – a few months before we got married.
Photo: Steve Fairnie

40th Birthday at Tamarisk, Chorleywood 1997.

The Spice Girls. Front: Emma, Pete McCamley, Melanie.
Middle: Geri, Melanie, Victoria. Back: Bob Grace and me.
Photo: Courtesy of Bob Grace

Misha and Jodie with Natasha Bedingfield in our old
kitchen, March 03.

Misha, Jodie and me with Sting and Kipper backstage in Paris, June 04.

Max (my dog), Jodie, me, Misha and Nicky the day before I proposed.

Verlon Battle – the love of my dad's life –
a beautiful soul.

NB with Engelbert Humperdinck at Air Studios.

Recording with Nashville's finest. Front row: Gary Barlow, Jane Birchall, Eliot Kennedy and me.

Jodie relaxing in Brittany aged 11.

Misha going to her first prom aged 14.

Nicky and the girls at Maenporth Beach, Cornwall.

My family – at home in Chorleywood.
Photo: Florence Macauley

At the NSPCC Ball with Nicky.

NB with Simon Cowell in Los Angeles.

With my best mate Ian Slade.

With Bryn Haworth 30 years down the road.

NB with Michael Ball.

With my dad in Cornwall.

NB with a baby at New Hope Uganda.

theatre, she had a total of nine different drains, tubes and wires going in and coming out of her body.

This time round, my boss was not quite as sympathetic with my taking time off from work, which created a little tension. What it did for Lynn, though, was make her feel more complete. For example, she could wear V-necked tops again and a swimsuit without feeling self-conscious, which was a great bonus. However, it left her with yet another massive scar zigzagging across her stomach.

After that we had a great run of health, success and a fabulous quality of life. We were happy. The kids went to a fantastic school. We were able to have wonderful holidays at Phil and Gen's villa *Casa Pacifica* in Mijas, Spain, on a pretty regular basis. And when we weren't relaxing there, we went down to Cornwall, where my dad and Verlon were living, to spend time with them during the school holidays.

The only fly in the ointment was my mum. Our relationship had become more and more difficult over the years as she continued to destroy herself with alcohol. Since the age of thirteen, when I really became aware of how much she needed help and looking after – at times effectively parenting her – things had been consistently tough. We'd done Alcoholics Anonymous, The Samaritans, social workers, the church, hiding the drink, trying to drink with her to understand, and numerous hospital visits after her attempts for attention and trying to exit this life. And now, twenty-six years after I first realised Mum had a problem, the madness had to stop. I had more important things to worry about. They included a wife surviving cancer and two young children to protect, who could now understand the drunken, broken, bitter bile that would be left on our answer-phone.

Something had to give. So I wrote Mum a long letter. I told her how much I loved her, how we *all* loved her, and how I hoped and prayed that one day she'd lay the bottle down. I explained how it wasn't fair to Lynn or the children to expose them to all this stuff. I said we'd changed our number, and that in future she could not call us but we'd call her.

She ended up in Hallamshire Hospital, Sheffield. I used to ring up to speak to the staff nurse. I'd hear Mum screaming in her madness in the background. I think she basically lost her mind towards the end.

Finally, I got the call I never wanted.

'Your mum is dying, you should come and see her,' said the duty doctor.

That weekend I drove up with Alan Stokes, one of my best mates, while Lynn looked after the girls. We got to the ward where Mum was, but when I finally found her she was barely recognisable.

Her little face and beautiful porcelain skin appeared to have shrunk. She was tiny and struggling to breathe. Alan sat outside the room, quietly praying.

'Mum,' I said, 'I love you, I'm sorry and I forgive you.'

I held her hand, but there was no acknowledgement from her. The next day I went back again and she appeared to rally a bit. I wasn't aware that she knew I was there, though. Later on, Alan and I drove back down the M1 to Chorleywood.

I was sitting at my desk in the Windswept office on Monday morning when I got the call.

'I'm very sorry, Mr Battle,' said the caller, 'but we really don't think your mum is going to make it through the day. Can you get here as soon as possible, please?'

I leapt in the car, drove to Chorleywood, deposited Misha and Jodie with a very kind neighbour, and Lynn and I raced up the motorway. When we got there, Mum's breathing was incredibly shallow and had developed a death rattle. There were what looked like pink foam lollipops in a bowl, which were to give her some moisture. We did our best with these, but it was useless.

Her best friend came and said goodbye, very distraught. A while later, with me and Lynn at her bedside, Mum died. As soon as I knew it, I got up briskly and walked away. One moment, Mum's spirit had been present with us, if only in a very frail capacity. The next she had gone. All that was left was a bag of bones.

Mum, and all her struggles, bitterness and sadness, had left. Only now would she be made whole again. I never went back to the hospital and I never went back to the house in Stainton Road. It was over.

The funeral was very, very sad. What can you say about someone who dies in such a tragic way? Nothing. What do I grieve over and miss the most? The opportunities she could have had with her grandchildren.

17

OH GOD, NOT AGAIN

I was in Santa Barbara, California (I know what you're thinking, 'it's a hard life'), on a company conference with our US and Japanese companies. This was something which took place every year.

Normally our Japanese boss, Ichi, would fly in for the entire conference. This time, however, he only came for the one night. During the course of the evening, he took me aside and thanked me for all I'd done for the company.

'It's a pleasure, Ichi,' I said, 'thanks for the gig.' And off he walked.

By the time we got back to the UK, I'd sussed what was going on.

'Bob, if we're for sale, can I go with a cheque, please?' I asked. It had all stopped being fun.

'Uh, OK, but I don't think we are,' said Bob.

By Christmas, however, it was all apparent. Then Evan, my American boss, and Bob Grace did a very classy thing. Knowing we were on the blocks to be sold, they re-upped my deal for two years firm. In the August of 1999, 90 per cent of Windswept was sold to EMI Music Ltd. I walked out with a cheque to keep the wolf from the door for some time, and went home to work out what we were going to do next.

In reality, nothing happened for two months. I started to panic a little. I'd given away 10 per cent of my settlement; having benefited from other people's love and generosity, I feel it's right to do that. Plus, it's a sound biblical principle.

Then in the October, I had a phone call from my friend Peter Barnes at Plangent Visions and then another from my other buddy Nigel Elderton at Peer Music Ltd. Before long I was back in business, consulting. I also got to work with my old mate Chris Briggs, (who I'd first met when he worked for A&M Records), helping with the song selection process for a Joe Cocker record on EMI.

Leeds Levy at Chrysalis Music in Los Angeles was prepared to fund a joint venture for me, as was Simon Platz (whose father David I'd been signed to when I was in Writz) at the Bucks Music Group in the UK. I signed a couple of writers to my fledgling publishing company, Star Street Music Ltd, and also picked up the rights with Simon to 50 per cent of the songs on the new Human League album. It was all going swimmingly. Wasn't it?

In summer 2000, Lynn and I went sailing with Ian and Annette Slade round the Ionian Sea in Greece. It was eventful, in as much as on day one the rudder snapped and we ended up adrift and way behind everybody. The guys from the sailing company, however, responded quickly and we made our way to Abiliki Bay. There we decided to drop anchor and Ian and I swam to the shore. Once there, though, we found to our alarm that the boat's anchor began to drag and it literally started to float away. The girls, who'd been swimming round it, got on board fast but weren't really equipped to helm it.

'Don't do that or you'll kill us both!' Ian called out.

So we tried to swim back to it. The problem was, any strength I'd had seemed to abandon me. I ingested way too much salt water and was fighting for my breath as I struggled to get back. Ian eventually managed to get me back to the boat by getting me to float and not expend all my energy, and by keeping me calm. When I got back, I had to be lifted out of the water. If Ian hadn't been there, I might not be here now. So much for day one!

I love swimming. I have scuba-dived in Maui, Hawaii and seen some amazing and beautiful creatures on the ocean floor, so I'm no slouch. But on that day, I got caught out. You have to respect the sea. That night I rang home. I felt like I'd had a little brush with death and I simply wanted to hear Misha and Jodie's voices.

Then one day, while out walking through the coastal port, Fiskardo, Lynn fell over and winded herself. It took her about ten minutes to recover. When we got back to the boat, Annette, a doctor, recommended that given Lynn's history, she should have a check-up when we got home, just to be on the safe side. So a couple of days after arriving home, off we went to Harefield Hospital. They recommended that Lynn have a small operation to look at her windpipe, and then an X-ray of her lungs.

A few days later we went back for the results. I remember we were kept waiting until the very last appointment of the morning. All the while, we sat there hand in hand, hoping and praying that we'd be OK. We figured if we were the last appointment, it had to be good news; otherwise why keep us waiting?

Then the doctor told us the results.

'Shit,' said Lynn, when the doctor had finished. And she hardly ever swore. Well, what would you say?

The cancer was back. And it was bigger, nastier and more virulent than before. I can't remember exactly, but I think I rang Phil and Gen (who were either at home with the kids or who must have arrived pretty quickly). And I told them.

Over the years, I came to hate the phone calls to Phil and Gen. I knew that what I told them on the phone from the hospital would break their hearts yet again, something I understood only too well. I loved them, and I loathed doing it.

When we got back, Lynn sobbed with her mum and dad. I went briefly to my log cabin in the back garden, closed the door, and screamed at the top of my lungs. It was unearthly, primal, and full of fear. If I felt like that, just how did Lynn feel?

We told the children. That was one of the hardest things I've ever had to do. They asked for the first time the question that was to become a regular feature of our talks.

'Daddy,' Misha would say, 'Mummy won't die, will she?'

'Well, sweetheart, Mummy's got this medicine to take, which will help her fight the cancer and smack the cancer on the head, and we should pray that happens, and for God to heal her.'

'But she won't die, Daddy, will she?'

'She is going to do her very best to be here and be with us and beat this disease, darling,' I'd say, while every sentient part of my body was dying inside.

The one thing I'd always promised myself, given my own childhood, was that when I married I would marry for life, and that my kids wouldn't have to go through the pain of divorce. Little did I know that they would have to endure something far worse. I had to be strong for Lynn, for Misha and Jodie and for Lynn's family.

Once again, Lynn started more chemo and radiotherapy. Her doctor at Mount Vernon Hospital, Northwood, was a gentle Greek man called Dr Makris. The treatment, care and attention both he and his staff gave to Lynn and me was practical, loving and beyond excellence. The back up from the Lynda Jackson Macmillan Centre was equally breathtaking.

I am very grateful to everybody there for the help they gave me at that time, but especially to Lynda Hannam and Lloyd Allen, my counsellors, who between them provided a safe place for me once a week on Friday for a couple of hours where I could get some respite before going back home to look after Lynn. Sometimes when I got there I would just sit there numb, unable to say anything. At others I'd be this bouncing, babbling person, clearly on the edge of losing everything. But it was my sanctuary.

At this time I was still acting as a consultant to a couple of music publishers. But I didn't feel I could guarantee to be there for them, because I never knew how Lynn was going to be. In the early days she appeared at times quite well, and I could crack on with trying to earn a living. However, from time to time, things would dip and I never knew when that was coming. When the dips came, my first responsibility was to Lynn, Misha and Jodie, but I didn't feel good about letting my colleagues down.

I rang my friends – Peter Barnes at Plangent Visions Music Ltd and Nigel Elderton at Peer Music Ltd – and they both effectively said the same thing. They told me not to worry, and they let the consultancies run their course, something for which I will always be incredibly grateful.

My friend Adrian Reith rang up one day and offered to set up an anonymous fund to help us survive while I looked after Lynn. I thanked him but didn't feel then that it was necessary. Some other friends of ours, Wyatt and Liz, were helping us to survive and not only that, God bless them, but also were sending us £30 of organic produce once a week.

We played a game of tag with the cancer in Lynn's lungs. Sometimes after treatment it would appear to have shrunk. At other times it would be larger. Lynn had a line put into her arm, through which the drugs were administered. We had to keep this clean and flush it out regularly to help prevent infection. I learned how to nurse. I had a lot more to learn.

Throughout all the treatments, and there were many, she fought valiantly, courageously, like a lioness fighting for life so she can watch her cubs grow up. I can honestly say I have never seen such bravery. Even now, remembering her and the pain she endured, I cry when I think about all she had to put up with – not just the physical, but also the mental and emotional anguish.

'You lose me, but I lose all of you,' she once said to me.

In writing about Lynn and the cancer I might be opening old wounds for some – certainly for myself. But I believe it is so important for this story to be told. My hope is that it might inspire others to be brave – and to believe that there can be hope for the future and also that people can and do get healed through going to God in prayer.

When we got the news the second time round, we obviously didn't want it. Cancer is not a club that everyone wants to join. Our prayer was simply this: 'God, if we have to go through this, don't let it be in vain, may people come to you.'

It was, at least, one prayer that was going to be answered.

In 2001, just before Phil and Gen's wedding anniversary, we discovered that the cancer had grown around the vena cava going into Lynn's heart. Her whole body swelled, including her beautiful face. Still she insisted on attending her parents' golden wedding celebrations. She could have died at any moment. But she was determined. And if Lynn was, so must I be. She pulled it off. But the process and people's concern, expressed privately to me, was heartbreaking.

'We've set up the fund to help you, don't argue!' said my mate Adrian in summer 2001. I didn't. And although I've been able to bust a couple of people involved, to this day I still don't know who they all were. But if you're reading this and want to come out of the closet, well I'd love to say 'thank you' face to face.

18

JOURNAL OF A HURTING HEART

From here things get a little random, in the form of scattered emails, rants, prayer requests. My dear 'adopted brother', Martyn Barter, who talked to me every day, heard me laugh, cry, and regularly swear, has kept these messages and recently gave them to me.

They document the next two years as I try and describe the journey. What I see now, reading them, is a man way beyond his life experience trying to do the best he can. Sometimes he fails, at others succeeds. I don't like him much. He is very far from perfect. So, for those of you who are of a nervous disposition, look away now.

Here is a song written on a day when I was feeling stretched beyond everything I ever felt before – something which was to happen time and time again. It's perhaps interesting to note that while purging my soul, I was able to write the concise email that follows, in what would appear such a calm way.

I CAN'T WALK DOWN THIS ROAD NO MORE

I can't walk down this road no more,
You've got to carry me, carry me Lord,
My heart is heavy and my feet are sore,
You've got to carry me, carry me Lord.
I feel betrayed, can't get no rest,
Been out walking in the wilderness,
I ain't no saint, I'm a sinner for sure,
I'm desperate for the truth not a sinecure.
I can't walk down this road no more . . .

Yeah you've got the power, you've got the look
Whatever it says in your Big Book,
Your body was broken, now we are too,
Come on fix us up Jesus, fix us up real good.

I can't walk down this road no more . . .

Well Yahweh, Jehovah, the great I am,
Come and make it real and heal this land,
We're desperate for a sign, we're begging for a cure,
Come right back through our front door.

I can't walk down this road no more . . .

Let the blood of the lamb, flow through this land,
Like a mighty river that has burst its banks,
Anoint the weary, refresh our souls,
Oh my sweet Jesus, come and make us whole.

I can't walk down this road no more . . .

'I Can't Walk Down This Road No More' by Nick Battle
Copyright © 2001 Star Street Music Ltd. Used by permission.

Sent: 25 September 2001 10.05
Subject: Lynn Update
Dear All,

Just to update you all, and ask those of you disposed toward a more spiritual approach for your prayers for us at this time.

As most of you know, following the operation to insert a stent (wire mesh) into Lynn's main vein (vena cava) she embarked on a ten day course of radiotherapy, which during the treatment seemed to be going very well.

However, serious radiation sickness has set in which means that the painkillers that Lynn has been taking have had little effect.

Please pray that the sickness passes and that Lynn's health stabilises. Also, and this is a big one, for Misha (9) and Jodie (7) who in the last few days are really starting to come to terms with Mum's cancer and the fact that she may not get better.

This is a huge thing for adults to deal with, let alone children, and this is one of the most painful things to deal with.

As most of you know I'm not the sharpest tack in the box so please pray that I would have the necessary wisdom and sensitivity and energy to deal with all of this.

Finally, if any of you want to ring please call me at the office rather than at home.

And finally, finally, I do want you all to realise that although at times things do look incredibly bleak WE NEVER GIVE UP HOPE.

Neither should you.

Thanks & God bless

Nick, Lynn, Misha and Jodie xxxxxxxxxxxxx

Throughout this journey I wrote as and when I could – or I would just burst if I didn't. Sometimes my words would just pour onto the page, bloody and visceral, at others they appear to just limp. Either way it was how I felt.

October 2nd 2001
My Brother Martyn.
No he's not my blood brother, he's my soul brother, confidante, Christian, friend.

My dear friend rang me and urged me to write things down as they happen.

So here we go . . .

As I write I'm recovering form a severe bout of simultaneous evacuation, tender and still a little feverish, my daughter Misha is now suffering with it.

We're hoping and praying that Lynn doesn't get it.

The last two weeks have been a living hell . . . first of all Lynn got acute radiation sickness, which meant she wasn't getting any fluids or solids that were staying down, more importantly the painkillers (co-proxamol/tramadol/Oramorph) were not working either, because they simply kept coming up. Lynn's throat was so sore that it was a ghastly experience just trying to swallow saliva, let alone anything else. It was extremely harrowing trying to nurse her through this as, although I'm good at most things, when it come to projectile vomiting I have to admit I'm not a champion

. . . with the exception of my 22nd birthday when I tried to drink 22 glasses of Pimms cocktail. It would have been all right but I couldn't cope with the volume!

So it's been tough. Tough, too, to watch Misha and Jodie come to terms with the reality of Mum's cancer in glorious Technicolor.

One week ago at 7.30 in the morning Jodie piped up with, 'Daddy, if Mummy dies, you won't marry again will you? Because I don't want you to, if you do it will remind me of Mummy.'

These conversations are carved into my heart.

My response was, 'Daddy is dedicated to you, and Misha and Mummy, and Mummy will always be your Mummy.'

Not great I know and some might say inadequate, but at that time of day I'm still pretty sleepy.

Later on Jodie told her mum of our conversation, 'But Daddy will get lonely,' she said.

When Lynn told me that, she also told me how far she had come on her own journey.

Let us not forget, there are several journeys here. Mine which I am selfishly trying to write both as therapy, but also in the hope that it might be helpful to others and raise some cash for the future; Lynn's which is the hardest one of all as she says, 'You lose me, I lose all three of you . . .'; Misha's and Jodie's, both with their own unique spin on things . . .

3rd October 2001

It is so painful to watch someone you love suffer. Not just physically, but emotionally, spiritually.

There is no remedy.

Both Lynn and I are at the place where we believe God can heal, but will He choose to do so? It is so awful to watch her wrestle with this.

I am ashamedly pragmatic. And cry out to God, 'Come on then, come and have a go, if you think you're hard enough!'

All our lives we're largely taught that God can heal and that Jesus performed miracles centuries ago, and I know He can. My father was diagnosed with idiopathic red cell aplasia and given three years to live, twelve years ago.

So I know He can do it. SO COME ON! Surely a dedicated, loving generous, funny, wife, mother of two young children deserves to live?
Doesn't she?
God, if you're listening, HEAR OUR PRAYER.
Rwanda, Srebrenica, Afghanistan, Save Our Souls. Amen.
SAVE LYNN.
SAVE US
PLEASE!!!!!!!!!!!!!!!!!!!!!!!!
Words are not enough, tears are not enough, prayers are not enough.
And you Lord?
Are you enough?
SHOW ME.

10th October 2001
I am being tantalised and titillated by the possibility of hope. This is one of the cruellest things to have to live with.

Let me tell you a story. A week ago Lynn went to a special prayer meeting at our local church, St Andrew's. There a couple of people prayed for her healing.

Her oldest friend Liz was also there. When they came home Liz was ashen and Lynn shocked but ebullient.

I asked them what had happened and Liz said that when they had prayed for Lynn, that it had looked like Lynn was choking to death right in front of her eyes. Yet what Lynn felt was something trying to escape, and a great sense of relief when it finally did. The people praying claimed this was the spirit of pain leaving Lynn's body.

Now for the spookiest bit. Lynn has been on a cocktail of painkillers up to eight lots on any given day.

For the past week, not only has she not taken them. She has felt no pain. Do you know what I think?

I don't care what the reasons are as long as it works. If Lynn is feeling no pain, then thank you God.

Be it the power of autosuggestion or God at work doing what we've read about in the Bible, and been led to believe. I don't care. If it works I'm in!!

So now I dare to hope. It would be more comfortable to take a cheese grater and rub it extremely hard on my dangly bits.

You get the picture.
Thought you did.
Don't try this at home.

I sang this song at church one night. I was aware that our family's journey was being hugely supported prayerfully by St Andrew's. I think our vicar, Mark Stibbe, was aware that God could take and use this painful process in more ways than one. I hope singing this song blessed people, and I hope reading it will also inspire.

HEAR MY HEART CRY

Here in my heart, high on a hill, I meet with my God, who loves
    me still,
No matter what life may bring me to bear, I'll always meet with him,
Because I don't care,
After all I've been through, I will defy the things in this life, that
    shelter the lies
If I labour in vain, then when I lay down to die, all I will do is
    hear my heart cry

Hear my heart cry, oh Lord, hear my heart cry,
And when I'm done, lift me up through the sky,
Through the veil of your love, to your temple above,
Hear my heart cry, my Lord, hear my heart cry . . .

There are choices we make, and wounds that we carry,
There are things in this life that simply don't tally,
While I can draw breath I want to live, with you my Lord and all
    that you give,
High on a hill, for the lonely and lost I see my name carved on
    that cross,
I can't find words to say how I feel,
I can't express, what my tears can't conceal

Hear my heart cry, oh Lord, hear my heart cry,
And when I'm done, lift me up through the sky,
Through the veil of your love, to your temple above,
Hear my heart cry, my Lord, hear my heart cry . . .

Lord bless my babies, Lord bless my wife,
Lord bless the things I do to get through this life,
Jesus forgive me for the things I've done wrong,
Help me to get to where I know I belong.

Hear my heart cry, oh Lord, hear my heart cry,
And when I'm done, lift me up through the sky,
Through the veil of your love, to your temple above,
Hear my heart cry, my Lord, hear my heart cry . . .

'Hear My Heart Cry' by Nick Battle
Copyright © 2002 Star Street Music Ltd. Used by permission.

Do you know what? Celibacy sucks! Let me rephrase that.
Enforced celibacy in marriage sucks. This is all about just
that.

ABOUT THE SPLEEN
2nd November 2001

I have a confession to make. Women terrify me. Particularly tactile
women. Sometimes I feel like I'm a time-bomb waiting to explode.
Why is it when the female sex feel sorry for you they get all . . .you
know . . . cuddly.

It's not a friendly arm round the shoulder that I want . . . it's
good, honest, athletic, sweaty sex. That may or may not involve
whipped cream and a bottle of sticky champagne.

I'm a relatively young bloke (44) with the mental age of 22 who
hasn't made love for a year.

Surely the RNLI can send a lifeboat to rescue me?

Ah but of course they can't. I'm bound by vows of marriage
that take no account of how to cope with a wife with cancer, and
all that goes with it.

Does that sound selfish? Well tough. 'Cos it's my turn today.

And I'm pent up, unfulfilled on so . . . many fronts and angry . . .

There that's better, spleen partly vented.

FOR NOW.

I guess this was our Christmas card to all those who had been
loving and supporting us.

To: Adrian Reith
Sent: 19 December 2001 10:26
Subject: A MESSAGE FROM THE BATTLE FAMILY (To all our anonymous supporters)

Dear Adrian

Please could you forward this message on to all the relevant people.

Dear Friends

This is strange. We by and large don't know who you are, we've tried guessing but we don't really know.

However, we want you to know that what you have done and continue to do for us is, to put it quite bluntly, life changing.

We feel humbled, a tad embarrassed, hugely grateful, and finally after a long struggle of the, 'I am not worthy' type . . . acquiescent.

If we had to worry about survival with everything else going on it would be well nigh impossible to cope.

So thank you.

Life is blessed but at times this year has been brutal, nonetheless we have a lot to thank God for.

For the fact Lynn is alive, for the love and support of family and friends. As I write I find myself moved to tears at the depth of love that we're consistently shown, for the very fact that we are able to draw breath.

Why in our arrogance do we sometimes presume that this is our inalienable right?

So here we are, Misha and Jodie are coping amazingly well, they have tough times and tears (we all do) but we talk it all through. As they develop they seem to have their mothers grace and élan, and as a father it is a joy to see.

They also possess a finely tuned sense of the ridiculous. Always important when dealing with Dad!

Lynn's health is currently stable, she gets tired and sleeps during the afternoons (when she's not writing her book with Jodie's godmother Rachel on Child Stress). She has, however, little if any pain at the time of writing.

The reason being is that she had prayer for the pain she was feeling about ten weeks ago, since when she has really had only the very rare occasional twinge.

So we thank God for that relief.

I myself was diagnosed with Graves' disease last week, which I could do without, but is dealable with. Basically I've a hyper-active thyroid which means everything in my body goes faster than it should! I know what some of you are thinking . . . 'No change there then!'

I'm going back for more tests on 7th January 2002.

But we're still happy. After all we're together, and that's the best Christmas present we could have right now.

To you our dear anonymous friends, we send our love, prayers and peace for a Very Happy Christmas. And thank you, we don't know what we'd do without you.

> God bless
> With love from
> Nick, Lynn, Misha and Jodie
> xxxxxxxxxxxxxxxxxxxxxxxx

Looking at this now, I wonder sometimes how Lynn endured what she did.

From: Starstreet
Sent: 09 January 2002
Subject: LYNN UPDATE
Dear Friends

Just a brief update. We made it through Christmas, the New Year, and Jodie's 8th birthday on 4 January, and as I expected Lynn having made a Herculean effort throughout this period, is now suffering a bit of a dip in quality of life and health.

Currently her speaking voice comes and goes, and at times she has to resort to writing things down. While she is not in a huge amount of pain (thank God) this latest development is upsetting and frustrating. She has been back to hospital for X-rays, blood tests etc and we have a scan booked for next Monday. Her breathing is also laboured at this time.

We have been in difficult places before, and this is just another hill to climb.

Please pray that Lynn and the family have the wherewithal to cope. Thank you

> Love from
> Nick, Lynn, Misha and Jodie

And again . . .

21st January 2002
It's back.

Bigger and nastier than before. Along with it has come that uneasy bedfellow pain.

Physical.

Emotional.

Spiritual.

Today Lynn starts an 18-week course of chemotherapy. It is her fourth lot. I don't really know if she will survive the treatment.

We have made plans, wills, funeral arrangements, who Lynn wants to pray/speak/support . . .

As I type these words, life seems so pithy.

Empty.

Meaningless except for the children.

Hopeless except for God, and I swear even He's asleep on the job.

Where and when and how will it end?

In my heart I pray for healing, and if that's not possible for release, and I feel guilty contemplating that.

I have never felt anguish like this and I hope I never will again. Lynn deserves better than this, and the children too.

Even I do.

Run out of gas.

But I still will not give up HOPE.

Just how do you define courage? Perhaps this is as good as anything.

29th January 2002
There are two women sat in our kitchen. They both have cancer for the second time around.

They are bravely trying to piece together a book to help other mortals going through the journey.

One is undergoing radiotherapy. One chemotherapy for the fourth time.

It will take a miracle for them both to survive.

Still they will not relent.

This is true courage.

I was out with two friends of mine last night, one a policeman, the other a Captain in the Royal Navy. They remarked that people get medals for less than we're going through.

To my mind the real medal winners should not only be the patients but also the doctors and nurses who year in, year out, carry on giving care.

There are no real prizes on this earth for bravery, or for inspiring people.

The only prize we really want is health while we're down here. And restoration when we get there.

There of course being Heaven.

Looking at this list now, it can only have been through God's grace and love that Lynn did so very well. She was a tower of strength. I sent this as an attachment to the following emails on 3 February and 4 February 2002.

PRAYER SUGGESTIONS FOR LYNN BATTLE

'If you want to, you can heal me.' Jesus said, 'I want to.'

Please pray with boldness and faith. Here are some specific areas into which you might like to pray.

- The natural trend of cancer is to grow, to cause more symptoms that will eventually cause death.
  Please pray that this trend is reversed. That the cancer would disappear, along with all the symptoms.
- Right eye is drooping, due to the cancer pressing on the nerve. The natural trend of this would be for this to extend to the mouth and the whole right side of the face.
  Please pray for the restoration of the nerve and the eyelid and against any spread of droopiness in the face. (A word was given about this in one of the Sunday services in January.)
- The voice is going similarly caused by a tumour pressing on the nerve, which leads to the voice box.
  Please pray for complete return of the voice and against it going again in the future. Also pray that this voice will be used to the praise and glory of God.

- The last scan showed that the right lung was now malignant. The doctor even talked about removing it, but since this would not remove the cancer, which is down the centre of the chest, the benefit was considered marginal.
  Please pray for the next scan to be free of any shadowing to show that this lung is completely free from cancer.
- Breathlessness, making walking and talking difficult.
  Please pray for good healthy lung capacity – for praise and worship and not shouting at the kids!
- The tumours down the centre of the chest had shown to be growing from the last scan. This is causing difficulty eating and in particular drinking.
  Swallowing is difficult, resulting in frequent coughing fits when it doesn't work.
  Please pray that the swallowing returns to normal and that all the cancer in this area vanishes completely.
- There are two swellings at the bottom of either side of the neck, probably due to a build up of lymph fluid as a result of some malignant nodes.
  Please pray that these swellings go and the cause of them goes too.
- Skin rashes flare up from time to time and are red and raw, which are one of the effects of cancer and its treatment.
  Please pray for them to go completely and not come back.
- Sleep is elusive, partly due to the effects of the steroids and mental unease.
  Please pray for peaceful and refreshing sleep.
- Chemotherapy is given by injection, but Lynn's veins hide when they see a needle.
  Please pray that the nurses would be able to find a vein, first time, in which to give chemotherapy.
- Five more doses of chemotherapy to have. Once every three weeks, which will take until May.
  Please pray that the power of the Holy Spirit will be in these drugs and that God will use them mightily and for complete healing.
- The chemotherapy affects the blood, the immune system and the hair.
  Please pray that the bloods hold up, that Lynn would keep free from infections and hair loss.

- The first few days after the chemotherapy are pretty awful. Please pray for minimum side effects and for strength to endure.
  PRAY WITH FAITH AND THANKSGIVING.
  THANK YOU AND GIVE THE GLORY TO GOD.

From: Starstreet
Sent: 03 February 2002
Attach: Prayer Suggestions 30.01.2002
Subject: 24 Hours Of Prayer
Dear Friends,

Just wanted to let you know that our church is planning 24 hours of prayer/worship/fasting on Monday 11th February starting at 10.00pm and going through till Tuesday 12th at 10.00pm.

On the Tuesday there will be a specific time in the chapel at St Andrew's to which those of you who can make it are most welcome. It will last from 6.00 p.m. till 10.00 p.m. with folk able to come and go as they please at any point.

We will worship, pray, and listen to the Holy silence.

> The address of St Andrew's is:
> Quickley Lane
> Chorleywood
> Herts

If you need directions mail me back and I'll send them to you by return. In the meantime please find attached a list of specific needs for prayer regarding Lynn.

> Thanks
> Nick, Lynn, Misha and Jodie
> xxxxxxxxxxxxxxxxxxxxxxxx

4th February 2002
From: Starstreet
Sent: 04 February 2002
Subject. Fwd: 24 hours Of Prayer
Dear All

Please find to download specific prayer requests. I'm aware that we're all at different stages of some kind of spiritual journey here.

Some of you may believe in God some of you may not give a toss.

However we do . . . and we believe it is better to live with hope than without it.

To that end the 24 hours of prayer starts a week today at 10.00pm.

Thank you for your love, prayers and support.

Love from

Nick, Lynn, Misha and Jodie

xxxxxxxxxxxxxxxxxxxxxxx

This was inspired by a builder who came to our house to fix the roof.

RANDOM THOUGHTS – MARCH 2002

There's a big man on our roof fixing a leak. I don't know him well and have only met him recently.

He somehow knows about Lynn and I tell him the truth, times are largely good at the moment, but can be bad.

He looks deep into my eyes and quietly says, 'I will pray for you.'

It is shockingly humbling and I run to the cabin to have a cry.

The comfort of strangers . . .

An email about the hope of heaven . . .

From: Starstreet
Sent: 11 March 2002 9:35
Subject: BATTLE FAMILY UPDATE
Dear Friends,

Just a brief update. To be honest if I'd written a book about the last month people would not have believed me.

Misha fell out of a tree at my in-laws' and broke her arm . . . that is now healing up nicely although she is presently off school with flu type ailments. Jodie was rushed to hospital last week because she was showing a lot of symptoms of viral meningitis . . . which turned out to only to be a particularly nasty virus. Thank God . . .

Lynn has had gastric flu but recovered in time to have her chemotherapy last Monday . . . although it took five attempts to find a vein that was going to work . . . we also had an X-ray which showed that the cancer is stable. In fact the oncologist said that he might even be persuaded that it had shrunk slightly(!). Typically cautious words but encouraging nonetheless.

You might be reading this and go . . . just what is going on? Poor people etc . . .

Our view is this.

Throughout it all God has remained constant and our family, friends, church and community likewise.

When you are in the fortunate position of knowing just how much so many people love, pray for, encourage and support you, then you know you are truly blessed.

Finally and this may be a strange one for some of you and perhaps not for others.

Because we're literally on the edge of life and death at times here, it has given us a very precious perspective and it is this.

Quite simply this life isn't it.

It's about the next one.

This life is fantastic and a marvellous adventure, but if I could give you a present today to say thank you for friendship . . . it would be the gift of eternal life. For us that means a belief in Heaven, a belief in forgiveness through Jesus for all the times we've stuffed up (trust me I'm grateful for that one!).

The knowledge that we're never alone, that we can hold God's hand through the trials and tribulations of life.

That's it. And even though at times, the situation here is really ****, it is made bearable by God and the love and support of people like yourselves around us.

So thank you.

If any of you want to write/argue/respond to any of this please do.

In the meantime.

Thanks & God Bless You All.

Love
Nick, Lynn, Misha & Jodie
xxxxxxxxxxxxxxxxxxxxxxxxx

9th August 2002

Yesterday was Lynn's birthday. A day nobody bar us believed that she would see. Her typical response was to say how blessed she feels and what a privileged life she feels we as a family have.

We had as you might expect a teary moment or two realising, as we have too, just what we have come through this past twelve months.

The stent that was fitted into Lynn's main vein into her heart to allow the blood to flow freely again. The radiation sickness, the terrible response to morphine, and yet more chemotherapy.

The 24 hours of prayer back in February before which Lynn could hardly speak, or digest her food.

The subsequent reversal of fortune as her voice came back and her ability to eat and drink did as well.

Even as I write this today she can eat, drink and sing with the best of 'em, after all she is Welsh!

Our friends who have helped to keep us alive, in so many wonderful ways.

We all have a huge amount to be grateful for . . .

So thank you Lynn, and thank you God

xxxxxxxxxxxxxxxxxxxxxx

END OF AUGUST 2002

The delineation of despair, does not always happen at the time of great trial or pain. Rather it is more insidious and seeps into our subconscious heart and mind when we're not looking.

Left unchecked it can rack us till every sinew mental, emotional, physical and spiritual is stretched well beyond what 'normal people would call reasonable'.

It is in this place that I find myself.

Wanting to be worthy, to 'Do the right thing'.

And yet desperate not to . . . needing to perhaps live a different life, in a different place . . . oh for the children how I hurt when I realised my parents weren't happy . . . we on the other hand are insanely happy, so happy it hurts . . . Not like the cancer that my wife carries, rather a happiness that reckons on life ANY life being short.

So live it.

The only problem comes when you all would like to live it at different speeds.

I do not feel the need to cram 120 seconds into every minute of every day, or have to live with the stress that goes with such an existence.

And yet there is no choice.
I live with Lynn, and the children, and the cancer.
Or I don't.
There is no choice. AND I DON'T QUIT.

*   *   *   *

So here we were at the end of August, and as you will have read, I was in a very poor space. Lynn's health had deteriorated after her birthday and she was given shed-loads of drugs to make her feel comfortable, steroids to get her through the day. The cancer, during September, started to affect her brain and at times she would not be the Lynn/Mummy we all knew, loved and prayed would by some miracle survive.

It was not to be.

19

THE FINAL FURLONG

The sheer grind of day-to-day survival began to exact a heavy toll on Lynn. We now had oxygen tanks, downstairs in the lounge, upstairs in the bedroom, with spares in the garage, and a nebulising machine which she used to inhale liquid into her lungs to try and aid her breathing.

She was very poorly. Yet she continued to smile, and take even greater joy in Misha and Jodie. A hospital bed was installed in the lounge. Lynn resolutely refused to use it. I loved that.

I tried to convey to Lynn just how much I loved her. When I felt words failing, I would massage her feet with oil, while she sat in front of the television with the family, fighting just to breathe. At other times, I would just sit quietly and hold her hand, screaming internally at God to make her better. Even then she was so incredibly ballsy and defiant. What an amazing woman!

At Christmas she was too poorly to go to church. So our vicar, Mark Stibbe, came to give us communion in our lounge before he had his Christmas lunch. Lynn sat there holding my hand, and my dad and Verlon knelt on the floor. We were all extremely emotional.

I guess deep down we knew it was probably her last Christmas.

From here on in, the nurses were with us 75 per cent of the time. Lynn's mum and dad, Gen and Phil, were also taking every opportunity to be with their precious middle daughter. I have not always been the easiest person to be around. Believe me when I say that is an understatement! But Gen and Phil have shown remarkable love, tolerance and amazing grace throughout all the time I have known them. I only hope I can develop that kind of selflessness, as I get older.

On the evening of 19 February, Lynn managed to convey her final thoughts to me, about what she wanted to happen. We had been preparing ourselves for a long time, and really there was nothing we hadn't said to each other, but there was some stuff that she still wanted to sort out.

Even then I believed that 'The Comeback Kid', as I'd taken to calling her, was going to pull through again.

'Don't worry,' I said, 'you'll be OK. We've been here before.'

In the last six months, instead of saying 'I love you' – which sounded so woefully inadequate – I had taken to saying to her and to Misha and Jodie, 'Everything'. It was so complete, so total.

'Everything,' I said.

'Everything,' she responded, managing a smile.

The following day, my wonderful wife, who had fought so courageously, faithfully, and valiantly against all the human odds for so very long, died in my arms, surrounded by her family.

Her last words were to her beloved daughters, Misha and Jodie at 9.30 that morning.

'I love you both.'

By late afternoon she fell asleep in my arms and went to be with Jesus.

Her struggle was over.

20

THE LUNATIC HAS TAKEN OVER THE ASYLUM

Lynn's funeral was amazing. That is, if it can be described as such. Friends flew in from all over the world to say 'goodbye', even from as far away as New Zealand. Misha played an exquisitely painful piece of music called 'Mummy's Slumbers' which she had composed especially and Jodie spoke straight from the heart. She was eloquent and confident just as her mum always was. Misha was only ten and Jodie just nine, and they were absolutely awesome. What on earth they must have been feeling, I just don't know.

St Andrew's was crammed to the rafters. Lynn was carried in by six men to The Waterboys playing 'The Whole of the Moon', and was carried out to 'As' by Stevie Wonder and 'Somewhere Over the Rainbow' by Eva Cassidy. Mark Stibbe, who'd flown in on the red eye from the States, spoke with great tenderness and love. Somehow he managed to hold it all together. Dave Wheatley led the worship. Inspiring and fragile, robust and stirring, all the spiritual and musical elements seemed to align perfectly. Three of Lynn's closest girlfriends shared memories with us. Barry Kissell who'd been there at the very beginning of the cancer journey led the prayers. J.John read the lesson. I'd written a song for Lynn with David Grant to a backing track created by Mike Spencer called 'In My Dreams', and that was played.

IN MY DREAMS

Oh and I'm never gonna forget, no I'm never gonna forget,
So much pain is coming my way, walking wounded in a daze,
No shelter from the rain up in the sky,
Can't believe I'm in this place, tears are falling down my face,
My heart just keeps screaming, screaming, why?

In my dreams, time will heal,
In my dreams, you're with me
Don't know what you're playing at now,
Don't make no sense, no way, no how,
All this pain and sorrow for my family,
Don't want to stand in judgement here,
But it's not right, and it's not fair,
Tell me how many tears must I cry?

In my dreams, time will heal,
In my dreams, you're with me
I can't go on, I can't go back, this is the hardest thing to do,
When loneliness is driving me insane,
And now my life's an empty page,
And I know I'll never see your face again . . .

In my dreams you and I glide by,
Hand in hand with a love that will never die,
You know that everyday I won't forget the love we share,
Wishing you were still here,

In my dreams you and I glide by,
Hand in hand with a love that will never die,
I don't regret a thing, you're all that I was looking for,
I could never want for more

In my dreams, time will heal,
In my dreams, you're with me
If I could bring you back to me girl,
If I could bring you back to me . . .

I put my arms around the girls and we held our heads high for Mummy and for God. After the funeral service, the cortege then wound its way to Oxford, where the girls stayed behind at their grandparents' house. I felt it would be too traumatic for them to witness the next stage. The closest of the close went to lay Lynn's mortal body in the ground.

The only possible way I can describe the way I felt – and still feel when I recall it – is that it felt like somebody physically tore my chest open with their bare hands and ripped my heart out before stamping on it until every vestige of joy and life that I had ever known had gone.

That night Misha and Jodie, Dad and Verlon, Ian and Annette, Alan and Sara, Bev and Alan, and Stokesy – and not forgetting Suzy (one of Lynn's closest friends) and husband Michael – returned to Chorleywood. We celebrated Lynn's life and had a wake. We laughed a lot. We cried a lot. We drank a lot. And the next day we all had to get up and get on with it.

Without her.

The first six weeks, people were great and supportive. Then over time they had to quite rightly get on with their own lives. Dad and Verlon would leave me to get on with it for a couple of weeks and then come and stay to help. I guess I was like a toddler learning to ride a bike without stabilisers. Now and again they would need to be put back on.

My best friend Ian and his wife Annette were brilliant. In every sense they were the fourth emergency service. At times I was completely reliant on them. They came to know Jesus as a result of Lynn's journey and watching her faith and bravery as we struggled over the years. So at least that prayer was answered.

My other pal Alan was totally there for me. Along with Ian, he had helped to organise Lynn's funeral. He'd held me in his arms as I wept at the graveside.

'Who's going to look after us, Alan?' I said.

'We will,' he replied.

There was a Thursday night pizza crew who would take me out once a week to give me a break: the Fabulous Barter Boys, Martyn and Darrin. While all this was going on, my pal Phylidda would babysit Misha and Jodie and provide invaluable mature female input into their young lives. And then there was David and Carrie Grant, Bev and Alan Sage-Smith, J.John and Killy, Mark and Alie Stibbe, Simon Hill, Tony Swain, Mark and Ann Morrison, Tim Woodcock and Hugh Goldsmith . . . All of these people saw me, hung out with me, some prayed with me, some wrote songs with me, while I was a complete basket case. They accepted and loved me. They accepted the kids and loved them, and they still do. There were the Mayos, Wroes and Reiths, who endured one of my more bizarre and surreal dinner parties, where I babbled and prayed incoherently while cooking a pad Thai, in between bouts of sobbing. And of course, Lynn's mum and dad, her sisters Sue and Sian, who were there for me even though all had a colossal journey of their own they had to endure.

So the lunatic had taken over the asylum. But what was going to happen next?

21

THE GRAVEL ROAD

I decided not to work for the first year. I was able to survive largely through having written some 'sound beds', which are like jingles that you might hear in the background while the news, weather or traffic information is being broadcast on the radio. That brought in some income. It was just enough to live on.

The girls had school dinners. So, in the evening, we generally had toasted sandwiches with cucumber, tomatoes and crisps or pasta or pizza. I'm afraid that I didn't do a very good job on the food front. But we got by.

I wrote songs with my pals Tony Swain, David Grant, Hugh Goldsmith, and Tim Woodcock. I even wrote one with Natasha Bedingfield, who was really lovely and kind to the girls. But not a lot happened. In retrospect, a lot of it was therapy.

My day would go something like this

7.30	Get up, make the girls' breakfast.
8.30	Take them to school.
8.45	Walk the dog/pray.
9.30	Sort out bills/domestic stuff.
10.00	Try and write a song/words etc/shop for food.
12.30	Lunch, normally a bowl of Heinz chicken soup and a roll.
3.30	Pick Misha and Jodie up from school.
4.00	Homework.
5.00	Toasted sandwiches/pizza/pasta.

Occasionally, I would go to a little guitar shop near High Wycombe or to John Lewis' to window-shop. But largely I was in the bottom of the grief pit trying to work it all out. There are many days that I haven't been proud of in my life, but there was one day when I completely lost it. And in retrospect I find it funny.

David Grant and I were writing a song. I was trying to record David's vocal in my studio, which was then in a log cabin in our back garden. Max, my little Schnauzer dog, would always sit outside the door keeping guard. In fact, since Lynn had died he had scratched himself so badly that he had suffered from an open wound one-and-a-half inches in diameter which had only just healed.

In a sense, we came to depend on each other a little. I'd babble on to him once the kids had gone to bed. He, in turn, followed me everywhere. But on this particular day, he wouldn't stop barking long enough for us to complete a vocal take.

I snapped and swore at the dog. I suppose the words I used were a bit over the top. David started laughing . . . and so did I.

In essence I told the dog to go forth and multiply, to stop his incessant whinging while also questioning who his father was.

People in extreme situations, often say and do extreme things. Christians are not immune to this process. Several months of pain and fury had erupted, all because my dog barked. And in a stream of abusive invective, my pain and hurt spewed forth. I'm not proud of it. But it is real. And Jesus does real.

In the evenings we watched loads of films and soaps, not ideal I know, but we were just trying to get through it. Then at about 9 p.m., I'd put the girls to bed. This could take anything from twenty minutes to over an hour. I used to say prayers and hold them until I thought they were asleep and then creep out of the room. But quite often we would have long periods of talking, and tears about everything that had happened and was continuing to happen to us.

I'd then tiptoe downstairs and open a bottle of wine. Then the next day we'd do it all over again.

In the summer of that year – and still rolling around at the bottom of the barrel – I was so incredibly lonely and I met and went out with someone for a short while. She is a lovely person. But it was entirely inappropriate to be dating anyone in the circumstances. As anyone who has lost someone close to them would know this is the case, and my regret is causing her and, more importantly, my kids, pain through my own selfishness and inability to see what my very best friends could. Would I listen to them? No. Stubborn as always. Wrong, wrong, wrong.

In October 2003, my pal Tony Swain, who was then consulting to Universal Records, came to see me. He asked if I'd ever considered returning to making records again, as there might be a gig coming up at The Decca Music Group.

I said I quite liked the idea. But I was a dad first, and everything else came second. I think Tony managed to persuade the president of Decca, Costa Pilavachi, that I might be a viable option. In any event he rang and I met with Costa, who is one of the great gentlemen of the record business – funny, urbane, and sophisticated with an incredible network and knowledge of classical music.

The deal was to take about six months to complete before I started work. During this time the first anniversary of Lynn's death came round – all too quickly. At this point, I'd met another lady, someone who I really genuinely liked. I sat in the church where I'd got married to Lynn, with a bunch of friends, listening to music and alternately crying and praying and letting it all out, the lady texted again and again and again . . .

The following night I saw her and we talked and talked. There comes a time where you kiss or you don't. Even though I found her enormously attractive, I simply couldn't. Wrong time, wrong place; and, as I now know, wrong girl. She nicked my heart for a short time. But I was only just starting to come out of the valley.

My pals in Chorleywood were wonderfully consistent, all of them just the best friends a man could ever wish for. There is one occasion which really sticks in my mind, though. My pal J.John – who for some reason calls me Nicolevich(!) – would regularly take me out for coffee and see how I was doing. I wasn't really doing well. I loved my girls but it was a gravel road – very lonely and very intense. One day, we found ourselves in Old Amersham.

'Let's pray for a wife for you,' said J.John.

So we walked into the massive old church in Amersham, knelt down in front of the altar and prayed. I will never forget that J.John loved me enough to do that.

It was Easter and I'd gone down to Cornwall to see my dad and Verlon. As usual on the Sunday, we'd gone with them to their tiny church in Perranaworthal, and we had laughed as, this being a rural community, the vicar had produced a series of chickens to illustrate his sermon. It wasn't unlike the *Vicar of Dibley*.

The next day I was having a leisurely get-up when I heard a commotion downstairs in my parents' hall. Initially, I chose to ignore it and then, against my better judgement, decided to go downstairs.

I am not a morning person. Any of my mates will tell you that. And I'm not particularly fond of meeting strangers first thing in the morning. However, as I went downstairs I saw two pretty girls, a brunette, and a blonde with gorgeous hazel-green eyes and a baby round her neck.

They were with their mother, who was chatting in a very animated way to Verlon and my dad. I thought the blonde, whose name was Nicky, was obviously married as she had the baby. But no, it was her niece and belonged to her sister Deb.

By further coincidence, the girls' mother, Cynthia, had been to school at Stockport Grammar forty years previously with Verlon. (I have the photograph to prove it!) But neither of them had known the other. Yet more spooky was the fact that the house that Dad and Verlon were in, was the house that Nicky and Deb's dad had bought for them and their mum Cynthia when they divorced.

My stepmother had been talking to Cynthia at church about me and the children. She was bemoaning the fact that, even though I was surviving, I was very lonely and had resigned myself to the fact that I wasn't going to marry again.

Cynthia had a daughter who was in her thirties and was yet to find the right person. So the mothers conspired, along with my daughters, with God, the architect of our lives looking on and no doubt smiling quietly to himself.

So it was a house of conflicting memories. Nicky and Deb got talking to Misha and Jodie, who were sharing their journey very openly, and also their sense of loss which they still felt about their mum not being with them.

'Were you as close as Misha and Jodie through the difficult times?' I asked Nicky and Deb.

'No,' they said, tearfully.

I also asked Nicky if I could hold the baby she was carrying. I like to hold babies, because you can quietly pray for them, give them some good stuff for the blueprint for their lives and ask God to bless them.

'Dad, can we have one of those please?' said Jodie, as soon as she saw me holding Katie.

'Sweetheart, talented as Daddy is, that is not something he can do on his own!' I responded. Jodie and Misha swear that I looked at Nicky as I said that. And everybody laughed.

'Now that's the kind of man I'd like to marry. He has a great relationship with his kids,' Nicky said to her mum later.

I gave her my business card. I know – not the height of romance – but what was I to do with my parents, my kids, her mum and sister looking on?

Come on! I was more than a little rusty in the art of romance.

The guys at Decca wanted to change things a little. Costa, along with his US boss, wanted to revamp the A&R direction of the company. The idea was to boost the classical crossover side, with more artists like Russell Watson and Hayley Westenra, while also exploring new horizons by signing singer-songwriters. The latter part of the job really appealed to me, the former not as much. I managed to construct a deal whereby I worked twenty-four hours a week, was still allowed to write and publish songs, and manage other people if I wanted to. I still didn't know how I was going to look after the girls on the three days I was in town working.

Then an amazing thing happened. Florence, the girls' piano teacher, suggested that on the days I was working in London she would look after them until I got home from work. This was such a godsend. As a mum with two kids, one in the sixth form and the other in his twenties, Florence provided a great female input in their lives at a crucial time. Along with the rest of her family, she provided a safe and unique environment for

Misha and Jodie to do their homework and be fed after school. But they were also encouraged to paint, sculpt, sing, trampoline and generally be the little girls they'd maybe forgotten how to be, all in a prayerful and Christian environment. They started to have fun again. It was wonderful to see, and proof of God's provision.

With my first pay cheque from Decca, I arranged for the three of us to fly to Paris to see Kipper who was on tour as Sting's keyboards player and musical director. We had the most brilliant time. Sting, who I suspect knew about our journey from Kipper, was particularly kind with Jodie and Misha. After the show I put Misha and Jodie to bed, and sat with Kipper in the bar of the hotel.

'I looked across at the three of you tonight,' said Kipper, 'and I really felt you were creating new memories. You all looked happy and it made me cry.'

And we were. We have been ever since. But we always honour the past.

Decca was initially great fun, until corporate politics intervened; however I can't possibly tell you about that. I did manage, though, to make a couple of records and had a wonderful time doing so.

My first signing, in my naivety, was Helen Hicks who fronted an outfit called the Honeyriders. She was a unique songwriter, charismatic and fiery with raven-black hair. She had just come out of a divorce, was a Christian and as broken as I was. We united in our common goal to make the Honeyriders successful. We brought in Andy Green who'd produced the Keane record. He did a fantastic job of mixing it. (Mixing, by the way, is the very exact science of balancing all the instruments perfectly so you can hear the song and all that it contains clearly.) I also introduced Helen to my friend Paul Crockford who manages Mark Knopfler. He tried incredibly hard, along with his team, to get things moving for the Honeyriders.

Two vulnerable people working together could have been a disaster, and commercially it was. Though I would love to elaborate as to why, I sadly cannot. Personally, though, we were mates. And after thirteen-and-a-half years of marriage to Lynn I learned to hang out with Helen, and not be intimidated by a strong single woman, but to also have fun. She is now happily married again to a lovely young man called James. One day I'd like to make another record with her; hopefully in better commercial circumstances.

Two other women were instrumental in my working life. They were Jacky Schroer and Jennifer Allan. Jacky is from Kenya and has fantastic musical taste. She is sultry and cool. She was a key person behind the global success of Hayley Westenra, and is a great pal. Along with Jen, our A&R co-ordinator, they saw me through a great deal. I miss working with them, and would work with them in a heartbeat again.

'Nick, do you fancy making a record with Engelbert Humperdinck?' said our head of business affairs, Mark Cavell.

The year before, Enge – as he likes to be called – had sold over six hundred thousand copies of his 'best of' album on the back of the John Smith's advert with Peter Kaye.

'Yes, I'd love to!' was my response.

So off Mark and I went to Great Glen in Leicestershire to meet with the legend that is Engelbert Humperdinck. The drive took just over an hour and a half, and we arrived at the gates of Enge and his wife Pat's Gothic mansion set high on the hill.

His office was vast. There were photos of him, with everybody from Elvis Presley to Dean Martin and Sammy Davis Junior, all over the walls. There were loads of gold records from seemingly every country around the globe.

At first he was shy. He asked us if we fancied going out for lunch, which in his case might have been breakfast. So we got into his Jaguar and purred down the hill to his local pub. We each had a pint of ale, and Enge had the full English breakfast. This was also washed down with a bottle of Rioja. Happy in the knowledge that we were now replete, we got back in his Jaguar and purred back up the hill. I proceeded to play him a selection of songs for him to consider, before driving back down south.

This process happened about three times, at the end of which we'd more or less chosen the songs that would make up the album.

22

AN ANGEL FLYING TOO CLOSE TO THE GROUND

Having started work at Decca and enjoying being back in the music business and feeling maybe my life was coming together again, the thought of Nicky kept nagging at me.

'No,' I thought to myself, 'you've made two mistakes, give yourself and everyone else a break, and wait.'

So I threw myself into my new role and did my best to try and forget Nicky and Cornwall and those marvellous hazel-green eyes. Round about July, though, somehow or other my dad sent me a couple of photos he'd taken when Nicky and her mum and sister had visited.

I looked at her happy smiling face and wondered . . .

'Dad, could you get me Nicky's phone number, please?'

Fancy having to ask your dad that! However, in double quick time he had got hold of it. Now here is where the stories start to differ. As Nicky's mum recalls it, I was desperate to get hold of her. That doesn't sound right . . . but I'd been hassling my father for the number, hadn't I? Anyway, as Nicky recounts it, her mum said something like this:

'Darling, I know I'm not supposed to ever give out your number, but do you remember Nick from Easter? Well, his dad rang to ask for your details and I passed them on. I thought it would be all right in this instance.' It was.

Nicky went and told her mates from church that night in the local pub. A few days later, she was down in Somerset working for New Wine, a Christian festival designed for families, when she received a text from me.

'Hi, it's Nick Battle here – do you remember me?' I wrote. Thank God she did.

I'd heard from my parents that Nicky was going down to Cornwall for a holiday after working at New Wine. As I was going to be down there anyway with Misha and Jodie, our parents had arranged – along with my daughters who were also in on the plot – for us all to have a family barbecue. Anxious about the whole thing, I rang Nicky.

'Hi, it's Nick here again,' I said. 'You do know that our parents have organised a family barbeque to get us all together? Well, I'm a little concerned about playing happy families. We've all been through a great deal, and I don't want anybody to get hurt. So can we please do the tap dance for the parents and then perhaps have a day where just you and I go out and spend time together?'

'Yes,' she said. And I heaved a sigh of relief.

The barbecue went well, although Nicky did invite her best friend along to ride shotgun, just in case! We ended up talking almost exclusively to each other all night with her parents, my parents, my kids and her best friend all looking on.

I was due to be with Nicky the next day in our original plans. But my friend Bev from the band Writz had just lost her dad. As the funeral was a couple of hours away in Torquay, I went to support her and the rest of the family. By the time I got home I was pretty tired but really looking forward to seeing Nicky. When I collected her, apparently the first thing I said was, 'I think there's going to be a significant exchange of information tonight.' Ever the master of understatement! But I wasn't wrong.

We ended up in the Norway Inn, Perranaworthal, a lovely little village between Truro and Falmouth. We told each other our life stories. Nicky had become a Christian in 2000. Prior to that, she had travelled the world visiting more than forty countries, working largely in sports television. She had just come back from a six-month discipleship course, working first in India and then Kenya with the Masai on the Tanzanian border.

I'll be honest. I found this stuff a bit frightening at first, as last on my list of requirements for a new wife was 'a missionary'.

(However, I'm slowly learning that what God wants for me is always the best.)

Her conversion had been a radical Holy Spirit experience, and she was a 'live wire' for God. I thought, 'She reminds me of a beautiful snowdrop that comes up in the spring, renewed and restored.' I, in faith terms, am more of a gnarled old oak tree. I've survived countless storms and some of my branches have fallen off! Well, that's what it feels like sometimes. But I have never stopped loving God or his Son, Jesus, who died for me. I've done more than my fair share of grumbling, though.

At the end of the evening and pouring our hearts and lives out to each other, I gave Nicky a big cuddle because I thought she really needed it. It was lovely. The rest of the week, we hung out together every day, but nothing physical happened. We would just walk and talk. Walk and talk.

On Friday, we sat in my car looking out across the water at Mylor Harbour, still talking – yep – just talking about everything. We talked about our expectations for life, what we both wanted to do in the future, where we thought God was taking us, and about the children.

'Of course we'll have to stay in Chorleywood,' I said, 'because after all the children have been through I don't want to add to any insecurity by moving from our community.'

'I know,' said Nicky quietly.

At that moment it was like the floodgates opened. I started to cry.

'My God,' I thought to myself, 'you're giving me a second chance.'

All this, and we hadn't even kissed. But we did pray about the future, and what it might hold. You know, I believe that is a really good thing. The world teaches us to get intimate physically very quickly. A lot of people do and I've been as guilty as the rest in the past. But what people really crave, and yet don't generally invest much time in, is emotional intimacy. Maybe they're scared or have been hurt too much in the past. But lives can be turned around. (It is my personal experience that God can – and does heal and restore broken hearts.) So it was, as the Americans say, 'all good'.

Nicky stayed down in Cornwall while I went back to London to make my record with Engelbert Humperdinck at Air Studios. And what fun that turned out to be.

I had chosen Simon Franglen to produce Enge's record. He is a master diplomat and consummate musician who has worked with Barbra Streisand, co-produced 'My Heart Will Go On' for Celine Dion and was the legendary David Foster's right-hand man for over ten years. (One of the world's greatest producers, Whitney, The Corrs, Celine Dion, etc, etc.)

We assembled a stellar team of musicians including Dave Hartley who works with Sting, Nick Beggs my old friend from Kajagoogoo on bass and Dave Geary on guitar. He can do in half-an-hour what I've been trying to do for thirty years! Not forgetting Martin Ditcham on drums and percussion.

We'd also taken great care choosing the songs, a lot of which were influenced by my childhood and the music my mum used to play me, in particular Nat King Cole's 'Let There Be Love'. Not only that, but also Enge chose to record one of the songs I'd been fortunate enough to write with my pal Tim Woodcock called 'Three Words Ain't Enough'.

Because he was still learning some of the songs as the rhythm tracks were being recorded, we brought in one of the backing vocalists, Andy Caine, to put down guide vocals to help Enge. However, there was a problem when it came to my song that I'd written with Tim, as Andy didn't know it.

'Nick,' said Simon Franglen, 'do you mind quickly putting a guide vocal on this for us, please?'

'Er, OK,' I mumbled before being pushed into the studio to sing. And then it hit me.

There I was, singing my song for Engelbert Humperdinck, Celine Dion's producer and a whole room full of some of the world's best musicians in what used to be Beatles' producer George Martin's studio . . . HELP!

I did my best in just one pass. But on a good day my voice sounds not unlike the bloke from the Human League. And on a bad day, it sounds like a fart in a space suit. I went back to the control room, more than a little embarrassed.

'It's hard, isn't it?' said Enge, without missing a beat.

We all broke up laughing.

Part of my job as the A&R/executive producer of records is to choose the songs, find the right producer and make sure the artist is happy and giving of their best. On this day, just as Enge was about to record his first proper vocal, I sensed he was perhaps a little apprehensive.

'Can I get you anything to drink? I said.

'I'd like some '64 cognac if you can, please?' he replied.

'OK, I'll see what we can do.'

Unable to find a suitable bottle of cognac, Air Studios, being the superb facility that it is, soon located a vintage bottle of Armagnac. Enge had a small drink and sang brilliantly.

Now much has been written about Enge's alleged womanising and he makes no bones about it in his autobiography, *Engelbert: What's In A Name?* His wife Pat even writes a chapter on how she feels about all that stuff.

However, throughout all the time I have spent with him, he was the consummate professional. He has a wonderful and unique tone to his voice, which for my money puts him up there with the greats like Sinatra and Tony Bennett. He was, and is, incredibly polite and courteous and his work ethic is second to none as evidenced by his touring schedule.

I also found him to be a deeply spiritual man with a dry sense of humour. So that's Enge, a curious mixture of a man with an incredible voice, and somebody I call my friend.

At the same time as I was making Enge's record, I'd also been approached to cut three tracks with Michael Ball.

I'd had a phone call from my pal Mark at Decca, asking me to attend a meeting the following morning with Michael, his management team and Brian Berg, MD of Universal Music Television. I duly turned up, and they were talking about compiling a 'best of' which they were going to call *Love Changes Everything: The Essential Michael Ball*. However, they also wanted to add three new tracks which Decca, as one of the other Universal labels, were going to pay for.

'You've made eleven albums so far and pretty much done everything,' I said to Michael. 'What would you like to do with these three new tracks?'

'Well, I'd love to record "This Is The Moment" from the Jekyll and Hyde musical and maybe a big iconic love song,' he said.

Later, Michael confided that he'd quite like to write a song, as well. In the end, we cut the Diana Ross classic 'When You Tell Me That You Love Me', written by Albert Hammond and John Bettis. Michael came out to my home in Chorleywood, and together with Tim Woodcock we wrote a gorgeous song called 'What Love is For' which I also managed to play guitar on.

My friend Tony Swain mixed the record at Air Studios with Paul Wright, at the same time as I was in the main studio recording with Engelbert. It was busy but an incredibly fun and rewarding time. It was a great privilege to work with Enge.

So far I have been blessed to record a total of three records with Michael Ball, *Love Changes Everything: The Essential Michael Ball*, *One Voice*, and the most successful album we've done together, *Music*, which sold just shy of a quarter of a million copies in this country.

Michael has been one of my favourite artists to work with. He has an incredible range, power and tone in his voice. He is a great interpreter of song, from big rock anthems like the massive Queen hit 'The Show Must Go On' to a beautiful tender love song like the Perry Como classic 'And I Love You So' and, of course, his incredible body of theatrical work from *Les Miserables* to more recently *Woman In White* for Sir Andrew Lloyd Webber. He is a very funny man, warm, loyal and self-deprecating and continually finds a great deal of humour in situations. For example, in 2006 I'd just returned home from Los Angeles and it was the weekend. We had a string session booked at The Angel Studios, Islington, London.

I was tired, but determined to go. However, having been away from my family for a week I was also anxious to spend time with them as well. So we all piled down to the studio. Michael was lovely as ever with Nicky and the girls. Misha in particular had a wonderful time with Nicky, sitting in with the orchestra and having to be as quiet as church mice as the musicians did their work. The session was produced by James McMillan who had been responsible for working with me on Michael's last album, *Music*. All was going smoothly. But I was feeling knackered from the jet lag.

'I'm going to go now,' I told Michael, after two hours. 'Do you think you'll ever possibly be able to cope without me?' I laughed.

Michael responded, quick as a flash. 'Well, my life will be a hollow, vacuous, empty shell without you,' he said. 'But, do you know, somehow I'll think we'll totter on,' he added, with a glint in his eye.

23

NICKY

Nicky and I started officially 'stepping out' in September 2004. Our first 'official' date was to go and see *Garfield* the movie, with the children sat either side of us. However, I did point out to Misha and Jodie that, as they'd come on *our* first date, that gave us permission to go on their *first* dates some time in the distant future. (As a dad, the more distant the better.) They thought this was very amusing. Not!

Nicky and I spent our time getting to know each other as boyfriend and girlfriend – but also as Nicky the potential step-mum to Misha and Jodie, and as a wannabe family unit. Nicky would come out to Chorleywood whenever she could. I remember one day coming home from work, to find that she had picked up Misha and Jodie from school and had cooked us all a family supper. It was so long since someone I loved had done that for me that I just burst into tears. A few weeks later we went up to Norfolk to meet Nicky's dad, David, and her step-mum, Steph. At some point I quietly took David aside.

'I think it's important that you know my story,' I said to him. So I sat him down and, for about ten minutes or so, filled him in. Then I added, 'I'm going to want to marry your daughter.' At this stage I hadn't worked out when I was going to ask her. But I'd also told Nicky's vicar, Mark Melluish. 'Is that OK with you?'

'Yes,' said David, without a moment's hesitation.

David is a big cuddly bear of a man, well over six feet tall. But he is also deeply emotional and I could see he was really moved. We had a manly hug, and for the time being said no more. We had a wonderful time in Norfolk for the rest of the weekend and returned home in time to go to the evening service at St Andrew's, Chorleywood.

That evening my friend and vicar Mark Stibbe was preaching. He is one of the greatest orators I have ever heard. Insightful, filled with the love of God and charismatic in every sense of the word.

'There are some of you here tonight that have been through an incredibly hard time,' he said, 'but now you are to walk in God's blessing.'

I took one look at Nicky. That was exactly how I felt. When we got home after putting the kids to bed, I decided to go for it and ask her.

'There's never going to be the perfect time to ask you this,' I said, 'but . . . will you marry me?'

'Of course I will,' she said, looking into my eyes. We hugged and cried and kissed.

'Aren't you supposed to be on your knees at this point?' she said.

So I went down on one knee and asked her again. And again she said, 'Yes.' We were so excited. We'd just put the kids to bed but I decided to wake them up and tell them the news. They bounded down the stairs, squealing and screaming with delight. They then proceeded to show us the drawings for Nicky's dress that Jodie had already designed for our wedding day! Nicky quietly and tactfully pointed out that perhaps scarlet was not her colour.

Next, we called our parents. Nicky's dad, David, was in the back of a cab in Spain when we finally tracked him down. There was unanimous joy. The Cornish crew – Dad, Verlon, Cynthia and John – were apparently up until two in the morning celebrating.

God had heard my cry from the heart and had given me a precious gift. Never underestimate what he can do.

In the months leading up to the wedding, we spent as much time as possible together, with Nicky staying over a lot of the time. This meant that I would sleep on a mattress in the lounge, while Nicky had my bed. The reasoning behind this was that what we model for our kids will affect their lives. Despite the fact that I'd been married before, I wanted, and we all needed, everything to be right. So we did what today is a very old-fashioned thing. Soundly biblical, though. We waited. Try doing that when you're forty-seven years old! Now if you don't consider yourself a Christian and you're reading this book, that part is not going to make sense to you. However, I always like to wait for Christmas Day before unwrapping any presents. It's way more fun, and can be quite tantalising in the process.

We decided to get married in March and set about organising our wedding. This was not an insignificant task. Both sets of Nicky's parents helped us with the funding of the wedding, which was just as well because it cost a packet. My father and Verlon also pledged their support by paying for our honeymoon.

However, little did we know as we entered the New Year of 2005, a tragedy was waiting just around the corner, ready to break us all again.

24

SEASONS IN THE SUN

As they were friends and co-conspirators anyway, Dad and Verlon, and Nicky's mum Cynthia and husband John decided to go on holiday to Spain. We rejoiced at this. We chuckled at how God knew that two little girls who'd gone to Stockport Grammar School forty years earlier, and who had never known each other, could be thrown together as friends and future in-laws.

I continued to work at Decca as an A&R/executive producer writing with Gary Barlow and Eliot Kennedy for a new artist, Joanne Birchall. We recorded a fabulous album in Nashville, with Nicky filming everything for posterity. But it never saw the light of day. The experience, though, was great fun.

It was an education for me to write with two great songwriters who had in their early thirties achieved so much. Gaz had excelled with Take That, his subsequent songwriter/production career and now Take That again. The song 'Patience' is awesome. I wish I'd written that with him. Eliot had enjoyed success with The Spice Girls, Celine Dion and his friend, Bryan Adams. (At the time of writing he is in Vancouver working on Bryan's new album. Now what I would give to lend them a hand with that!) After the success of the album *Love Changes Everything: The Essential Michael Ball*, I tried to pick up the option for Michael to make a new album.

'He is not a Decca artist,' I was told.

So along with Michael's then manager Brian Yates, we persuaded Brian Berg at UMTV, another Universal company – who knew Michael and understood his market – to pick up the option. He did so with great alacrity. We were all overjoyed when the album went gold.

I also recommended the tenor Alfie Boe, the jazz singer Madeleine Peyroux, amongst other talents, to the label. But it was becoming more apparent that whatever mandate I'd been given was being slowly eroded. Commensurate with this seemed to be that my boss, who I liked a great deal, was also undergoing what was to be a slow exit out of the company. I resolved to do the best I could, keep my head down and get paid, but it was a frustrating time. One day after lunch, Jen, our A&R co-ordinator, found me.

'Your dad's been trying to get hold of you,' she said. 'It's urgent. Here's the number of the hotel in Spain.'

I tried ringing, but couldn't get through. I rang his mobile but no answer. I ran down to the corridor to Carol Wright who was our head of international marketing, as she was fluent in Spanish, to try and get through to the hotel again. Still no luck. Then my dad rang back.

'Verlon's dead,' he managed to say.

I went into shock. I think I told my dad I loved him and asked him if he wanted me to come out to Spain. But thank God, John and Cynthia were there to help him. I rang Nicky straightaway and told her. My Decca colleagues Jen and Jacky were very kind. Jen quickly organised a car to take me home, and brought me a cup of tea while I waited. Jacky held my hand as I cried.

'It's not me. It's the kids. Not again!' I said.

By the time I got home, Misha and Jodie's grandparents, Phil and Gen, were there. They usually came from Oxford on a Thursday. Misha came home first, and I remember sitting with her by the piano waiting for Jodie to arrive so I could tell them both together, knowing that once again their little hearts would be broken.

I'll never forget the sound of their anguish. We held them, Nicky and I. We held them tight, and we sobbed our hearts out – all four of us. Then we went into the kitchen and did the same thing with Phil and Gen. Verlon was not my mum, but she was the very next best thing, a wonderful friend, and instrumental in bringing Nicky and I together. She had been enjoying her 'seasons in the sun', with her beloved husband

and two dear friends, sitting in the back of the car with Nicky's mum. But that lovely time was cut short when she had a heart attack and quietly just slipped away.

A beautiful spirit. The love of Dad's life.

We were frantically busy in the months leading up to our wedding. Nicky was working for New Wine and Sky Sports. I was busy at Decca. When we weren't at home looking after the kids, we were flat out organising the wedding.

Amid all this, after much prayer and deliberation we decided to sell both Nicky's home in Ealing, and our family home that I had shared with Lynn, Misha and Jodie. I think for all concerned it was the best thing to do. We would have a new life, a new start and a new home.

For me, what had been written in the Bible about God, 'restoring the years the locusts have eaten', was coming true. (For those of you who aren't familiar with this verse from the Old Testament, it means God restores good things to us when we've had bad stuff in our lives. See the book of Joel 2:25.) Don't get me wrong. I loved Lynn and the years I had with her . . . even the really difficult and painful times. But there was a very real sense that in order to look after her needs and those of the children, my own needs had to go on hold. And I'll be really honest here. I was desperate to reclaim them.

By the time we got married, we had managed to sell Nicky's property. But the family home was still on the market. So the night before, as Nicky went off with her grandma May, her mum Cynthia and Misha and Jodie to stay at a hotel in Ealing, I had dinner with my dad, John and my best man Ian.

The next morning the phone rang at 7 a.m. It was Nicky. There was a fire at the hotel. She was with the girls who were all OK – if in their pyjamas – but her mum and her stepsister Carol were missing.

'Bride's Special Day Goes up in Smoke!' I silently wrote the headline in my head. I prayed fervently that Cynthia and Carol would turn up, which they did ten minutes later. They had nonchalantly strolled outside with a cup of coffee. All was well. The small fire that had triggered the smoke alarm had been contained.

I could see it was going to be a very interesting day, to say the least. Then, life should never be dull, should it?

The sun was shining. It was incredibly mild and warm for the time of year. I was calm yet excited, knowing that this was my destiny and knowing that a new chapter of life was beginning. This was tempered with thoughts for my father on this day, and for others who might be missing their loved ones.

I was picked up by an old mate, Said. He drove me, my dad and Ian Slade to Nicky's church, St Paul's, Ealing. When I arrived, my pal Joanne Birchall was sound-checking and singing 'All the King's Horses', the song I'd written for Nicky with Gary Barlow and Eliot Kennedy. Here it is.

ALL THE KING'S HORSES

Changed my life everything I know,
I was looking for something I could call my own,
No shoulder to cry on, no kiss for my tears,
Where's all the laughter that used to be here,
Wanting my heart to believe,
Everything that my head can conceive . . .

That all the king's horses, and all the king's men,
Couldn't put my life together again,
I threw down my weapons and unclenched my fist,
You came along and I couldn't resist,
I know for sure I will never find better than this

Where were my friends, where had they gone,
I was ringing the bell, there was nobody home,
Lying in my bed, don't heal the pain,
And hugging a pillow, just don't feel the same,
How did you get my heart to believe,
All the things that my head can conceive . . .

That all the king's horses, and all the king's men,
Couldn't put my life together again,
I threw down my weapons and unclenched my fist,

You came along and I couldn't resist,
I know for sure I will never find better than this

No sleep 'cos the silence was too loud,
Needing, hoping, dreaming, that I'd found love,
Forever love, unbreakable love

That all the king's horses, and all the king's men,
Couldn't put my life together again,
I threw down my weapons and unclenched my fist,
You came along and I couldn't resist,
Nothing so far has come top of my list.
I know for sure I will never find better than this
No, no, no, better than this,
Better than this . . .
Better than this.

'All the King's Horses' by Nick Battle/Gary Barlow/Eliot Kennedy.
Copyright © 2005 Star Street Music Ltd./Sony-ATV Music Ltd. Used
by permission.

It was a wonderful service. I will never forget turning round to
greet Nicky as she came down the aisle on the arm of her
father to Stevie Wonder singing 'Signed, Sealed, Delivered'.
She looked radiant, serene and very beautiful.

The prayers led by Mark Stibbe were passionate, erudite
and filled with the love of God. First prize for praying, though,
has to go to one of my oldest friends, Adrian Reith, who quite
simply stood up and said: 'THANK GOD FOR NICKY!'

And I do every day.

My dear mate J.John – who'd prayed so faithfully with his
wife Killy that I might find a wife – spoke with tremendous
warmth, eloquence and a great deal of humour. Here are a few
quotes from his marriage speech to us.

About one wife who prayed:
'I pray for wisdom – to understand my man;
Love – to forgive him; patience for his moods;
Because Lord if I pray for strength, I'll beat him to death. Amen.'

One man asked God: 'Why did you make women so soft and
beautiful?'
God replied: 'So you'd love them.'
Then the man asked God: 'Why did you make women so illogical
and emotional?
God replied: 'So they'd love you.'

'I encourage you both to try and out serve one another.
It's said that you marry the one you love.
My advice is to love the one you marry.'

The marriage ceremony was led by Mark Melluish, Nicky's
vicar. He had welcomed her when she was really lost and yet
really drawn to the church across the road. It was a time of cel-
ebration. We honoured the past, celebrated the present and
walked forward boldly into the future.

The reception was held at Old Jordan's, Buckinghamshire,
in a 600-year-old barn.

Florence, who had been such a massive help looking after
Misha and Jodie, took the pictures; one of her many skills is as
a professional photographer. The atmosphere was like our
own private heaven with God, family and friends celebrating
the precious gift of love.

Speeches were delivered by not only the best man and
Nicky's dad David, but also Misha and Jodie. They spoke dif-
ferently but passionately about the journey we'd all been on,
and also about how much they loved Nicky. We all cried tears
of joy.

My dad, who had dreamt of celebrating this day with
Verlon, was very brave. I really felt for him. We all missed
Verlon, but felt very close to her.

David and Carrie Grant made a speech of sorts, like a multi-
choice *Cosmo* quiz tailored for us and the qualities we were
looking for in a perfect partner. It was very funny.

Nicky spoke with typical and effortless grace. She acknowl-
edged Lynn's parents, Phil and Gen, who we were delighted to
have with us on our big day. I said a few words. I spoke about
how beautiful my wife is; about how God helps us to recover and
restores us; how wonderful to love and to carry on celebrating life

until we draw our last breath; and how amazing that God brought us to this sacred place. The final word on this occasion, though, was from Ian.

'They're a couple meant for each other,' he said, 'and a family that's meant to be.'

Amen to that.

25

THE FUTURE'S SO BRIGHT I'VE GOTTA WEAR SHADES

A weird feeling came over me. It was as if I was being watched. Our wedding night at Hartwell House had been everything we dreamed it would be. But our honeymoon on Italy's Amalfi coast was becoming . . . strange. People were staring.

The penny finally dropped. An Italian restaurant owner told me I looked like the Neapolitan singer-songwriter Gigi D'Alessio, whose romantic ballads are popular across Europe. I immediately bought his records and discovered him to be a man who is impossibly handsome with a fantastic singing voice. Surely some mistake . . .

After that worry had been cleared up, we enjoyed our stay on the Neapolitan Riviera. We were staying near the ruins of Pompeii, in Positano, a region praised by Franco Zefferelli for its 'extraordinary beauty'. Tiny roads curve dramatically, and you can see lots of little caves and grottos. It was beautifully warm and we enjoyed the sanity of just the two of us being together with God, celebrating the essence of life itself.

We then flew back to England, which was eventful in itself, as we narrowly avoided another plane on the ground at Heathrow. Instead of coming in slowly and carefully to land, at the last minute our plane shuddered upwards, banking steeply. We were sat in a row of three. The Italian lady to our left was borderline hysterical.

What made matters worse, was that the pilot didn't talk to us for ten minutes. Eventually he apologised, explaining calmly what had happened, and that we had been put in a holding pattern. Half an hour later – which seemed like an eternity – we were on the ground.

As we disembarked I spoke to the two slightly camp male stewards at the front of the cabin.

'Please thank the pilot for getting us down safely,' I said. 'He has balls of brass and nerves of steel!' They tutted and giggled.

'Thank you for flying Plummet Airlines!' they responded.

No, they didn't, but I'm not at liberty to tell you . . .

That night we had dinner with Ian and Annette, before setting off the next day and driving slowly up to the Isle of Skye, staying in old fashioned country houses and inns. We had a wonderful time, just the two of us. It was lovely to enjoy the luxury of each other, and the rugged and distinctive beauty of the isle, without distractions. (It's something we still strive to do as we approach our second anniversary.)

Within a few weeks of our wedding we had an offer on our house. We managed to find a property just five doors down from my best man Ian and his family. To be honest, I was a bit concerned about living so close to a family who so ardently admire such a terrible football team as Chelsea. But you can't have everything . . .

Work at Decca continued, for which I was grateful. But with the exception of being A&R/executive producer on one track for Russell Watson (a Manchester United fan like me) for his *Ultimate Collection* – which did well – it was rather dispiriting. I was being paid well, but it was proving to be a difficult time.

Eventually my boss left the company (which we'd all seen coming) but nonetheless it was a great shame. As I was also nearing the end of my contract with them, in January 2006 I suggested that they pay me out and I would work from home. They agreed, which gave me time to approach my friend Brian Berg at UMTV about making another Michael Ball album, *One Voice*. Happily Brian agreed, and Michael and I reunited with James McMillan and began work in earnest. But there was another surprise in store.

One day, Jen, my pal from Decca, rang to say that a chap called Sonny Takhar had rung from Syco Music about 'songs'.

At first I thought maybe Sonny had heard one of my songs that I'd written. So I quickly rang him back, spoke to him, and a few days later met with him at the Syco HQ. However, that was not why he had called.

Sonny is the right-hand man for Simon Cowell, and runs Syco Music for him on a 'hands-on', day-to-day basis. Simon and Sonny were looking for somebody with the depth of experience of finding great songs to help them as they looked toward making new records for Il Divo and Westlife; they also wanted to introduce a stunning new act, Angelis. Sonny asked me to fly to Los Angeles and meet him and Simon.

Although I've known Simon since 1990, I wasn't keen to leap on a plane. I don't like flying. But more importantly, I didn't want to leave my wife of just thirteen months, or my kids. However, Nicky and I prayed about it and we decided I should go. So a few days later I was getting up at the crack of dawn to catch a British Airways flight to Los Angeles.

When I left, Nicky burst into tears as did Misha and Jodie. It was incredibly hard saying goodbye. But it had to be done. I guess having lost my mum, my best friend and then my first wife in quick succession, I'm very aware of leaving people behind and my own mortality. But everyone has to work, and this was a great opportunity.

It was a typically average English day. The weather was slightly overcast, as if mirroring my thoughts and fears. I arrived at the check-in desk.

'Gosh, you must be tired,' I said to the young woman behind the desk. 'What time do you have to get up to get here and do this job?'

'Three o'clock in the morning,' she replied.

'How long have you been doing it for?'

'About eighteen months. I'm thinking of stopping soon,' she said.

'I don't blame you,' I remarked. A few more minutes banter about whether or not I'd packed my own suitcase or been given anything dangerous to take to America, and I was on my way.

'Have a lovely flight,' she said smiling, and I left.

As I boarded the plane a couple of hours later, happy that I was flying Club Class on a long-haul flight, a stewardess approached me.

'Oh no, Mr Battle. Today, you're flying First Class.'

The lady who had checked me in had very kindly upgraded me. Thank you, God! Now, I love fine wines – particularly Puligny Montrachet – and to my deep and profound joy, I was able to taste this wonderful libation with my lunch later that day, as I lay on my sofa bed flying over the Atlantic Ocean.

On arrival in Los Angeles, I was picked up and taken to my hotel where I confirmed my meeting with Simon and Sonny for the next day. The atmosphere of the place was luxurious yet soulless. (Anywhere that charges you $10 for a bottle of water has to be taking the proverbial.) I didn't sleep too well. At four o'clock I woke, switched on my laptop and watched the *Jimmy Carr Live* DVD I'd bought back at Heathrow for moments like these. I chuckled away quite happily for ninety minutes and then caught up on world events from America's perspective on CNN.

At 6 a.m. I got up and went over my preparation for the meeting with Simon and Sonny, trawling through yet more lists of possible songs. I was listening to Brian Doerksen's song 'Faithful One', when I became aware of the atmosphere in the hotel room changing. I had been apprehensive about the meeting. Now I felt peaceful.

I'm not one for big 'Holy Spirit' experiences on a regular basis. But I suddenly found myself face down on the deeply luxurious carpet. I was aware of an inner voice.

'Don't worry,' said the voice. 'I've brought you this far. All will be well.' It wasn't audible. But the words very clearly came into my head. And everything was well.

Later that day, I took a cab to Simon's house. The last time I'd seen him was over six years ago. We'd both experienced serious life changes. I'd lost my wife. He had gained 'the world' in many ways. He had been successful before. Robson and Jerome were his first major breakthrough album act and Five had also done brilliantly. But now, Westlife had gone on to sell millions of records and he'd launched Il Divo who had, seemingly effortlessly, conquered the globe in no time at all.

Simon might be a major star here in the UK. But in the States there are billboards of him everywhere. He is the *American Idol*. He has his own film and television companies, and music corporation. It was a long way from *Lucky Seven Megamix*, a record he'd put together with Nigel Wright and which I'd promoted back in 1991.

How was he going to be?

He was just the same. Very polite. Very professional. Still smoking menthol cigarettes and still possessed of a phenomenal ear for a great song.

'You're looking well,' Simon said, smiling.

'So are you,' I laughed. 'Thanks for this opportunity. It's good to see you again. I appreciate it.'

I'd flown 5,000 miles for this meeting. My prayer was that he and Sonny would like some of the songs I'd chosen, and they did. It was an incredibly positive meeting. I came away really excited, although they did manage to double my workload in the course of one thirty-second conversation! That's OK though, because they kindly doubled the money.

I flew to Nashville where I met with a load of music publishers trying to find the 'lily in the dustbin' or the 'ruby in the dust'. I found a few gems. But on this occasion they were not the finest. One song, 'Live Like You Were Dying' stood out, but was too American, with its references to rodeos and Rocky Mountain climbing.

Back home, I sweated twelve hours a day, compiling everything that Simon and Sonny had asked for, with some extra information I thought they might find useful in the future. At the end of four months the task was complete. Simon rang one day out of the blue and thanked me for all my hard work, and told me that a couple of my song suggestions were being recorded by Il Divo. I was delighted that he and Sonny were happy with the job I had done. I was also pleased that he had taken the time to call.

The rest of 2006 I continued my work with Misha's godfather, Kipper. We made a fabulous record with Estonian rock act Thief, who sound a little like Talk Talk, with a dash of Duran Duran and Coldplay.

Kipper finished work on his Bang and Olufsen-sponsored solo album, *This is Different* on which he revisited 'A Thousand

Years' with Sting, this time with Israeli maestro Yechiel Hasson playing some sublime guitar. The record also features collaborations with Curtis Stigers, Richard Marx, Judie Tzuke and Mike Lindup from Level 42. I was particularly thrilled to be asked to co-write a song with Kipper which came out as 'We Come In Peace'. It's the story of every child that's born. We're all just blank pieces of paper waiting to be written on.

WE COME IN PEACE

> We come in peace, no malice here,
> We have no memory, we have no fear,
> We need your love, don't need no hate,
> We've got a good feeling this world's gonna be great . . .

> *'We Come in Peace' by Nick Battle/ Kipper/Tommy Blaize*
> *Copyright © 2006 Star Street Music Ltd./Kipper Music Ltd./Tommy*
> *Blaize. Used by permission.*

So I'd left Decca, had some success with a track on Russell Watson's *The Ultimate Collection*, made another Michael Ball record, consulted to Simon Cowell, managed Kipper and had begun work on this, my autobiography. The last twelve months have been a bit of a rollercoaster ride, but have been great fun too.

So what now? It is June 2007.

If you've got this far and haven't fallen off your perch through boredom, thank you! I'm fifty this year, but I don't feel it. My lovely young wife and I would like to add to our family, but only God knows. I'd like to write a song people remember for many lifetimes, like 'Somewhere Over the Rainbow', 'Fields of Gold' or 'Wonderful World'.

What's the greatest song written in the last five years? Well, there are two: 'You Raise Me Up', recorded by over 150 artists so far including Michael Ball, Westlife, Josh Groban, Russell Watson to name just a few, and 'How Great is Our God' sung by Chris Tomlin, which is an undiscovered gem outside of the Christian music scene.

I'd like to write something like that.

POSTSCRIPT: NEW HOPE

You know how your mates will ask you out for a beer or a curry? Well, Mark Stibbe came round over Christmas 2006. But this time it was a much more unusual invitation. 'Do you fancy coming to Uganda?' was the gist of it.

'What? You must be off your trolley,' I said. 'Why would I, of all people, want to go?'

But another voice joined him in support of his request.

'Come on, Big Boy,' said Ian Slade, 'it will be a laugh.'

'Don't tell me he's talked you into it as well!' I exclaimed.

'Yes,' replied Ian, 'Annette and I went out for a curry with Mark and Ali and talked about it. I think it's a great idea. We can really do something useful.'

Then my wife looked at me. When we were engaged I had made a promise that at some point I would go to Africa, ideally Kenya or South Africa, but Uganda?

I can never resist my wife so I said, 'I'll think about it.'

'Good, you're in then,' chorused Mark and Ian.

And from that moment, I was.

It came to pass that I found myself queuing up at Heathrow Airport on 25 March 2007. It seemed that we stood in a line for ages before finally boarding the plane. There was a lot of banter between us all. But I reckoned Ian and I were probably the most nervous.

Our feelings were calmed when, through God's grace – and, I suspect Ian's phenomenal negotiating skills – three of us managed to get upgraded. That meant that one of us had to stay behind. As the eldest, I was looking forward to a little comfort and felt reluctant to stay in the economy section. I needn't have worried.

'Don't worry, I'll stay behind,' said Dave Hill, our children's worker from church, with a selflessness that I was to come to greatly admire.

On arrival in Kampala, we were met by the team from New Hope Uganda: Jay Dangers, Keith McFarland and Dave Clay. The roads were teeming with life and dust. There were potholes everywhere. Those who had a method of transport, be it bicycle or motorbike, were carrying as many people and things on board as possible. We frequently passed people who had most of their family attached in some form or other to their bike.

Our driver, Dave Clay, took a back route. We saw people living on top of each other. Expectant black faces peered at us as we slowly negotiated the red dust roads. We struggled reluctantly to take photographs. I felt like a voyeur of poverty.

It was two hours of bumping and swerving. It took great skill to avoid other Ugandan drivers who don't care which side of the road they drive on as long as they avoid the gaping chasms in it. We arrived at Kasana, deep in the Luwero triangle. This was Kasana Children's Centre, New Hope Uganda.

It had been established back in 1986 after years of war during Idi Amin's rule which had taken 500,000 people's lives and left an entire generation of fatherless children. The centre was built on land that was a kind donation from Daudi Mukubira in 1986.

This territory has become a place where over four hundred children – some who live there and others who come from nearby villages on a daily basis – are loved and cared for, educated, given medical treatment and discipled (that is, taught about Jesus).

The boarders have no living relative willing or able to raise them. The day pupils frequently have difficult home situations which can and do affect their emotional and spiritual stability. There is a primary school, secondary school, a vocational institute, baby ministry, an institute of childcare and a Family and Kasana Community Church.

The children from the war years are now adults. So most of the kids who come to New Hope have lost one or both parents to AIDS. It is a place where the Father-heart of God is clearly in evidence.

Throughout the week, Ian and Dave did a superb job with the children, playing football with them and encouraging team sports and races. It may seem daft but they just love to play; primarily because, for some, that's still a novelty.

Mark taught and spoke passionately on 'The Father Heart of God'. I helped with the music, gave my own testimony and, along with Mark, prayed for anyone who needed it. A great number did. Unlike the UK, where people can be embarrassed to 'go forward' for prayer, in Uganda they are only too willing to enjoy an intimate encounter with God.

I went with Mark, Ian and Dave to the baby ministry. There were about ten children each with a tragic story of their own. We heard the story of Joy, who had been thrown into a pit latrine and left for dead by her mother. But two children's journeys have wrecked my heart forever. The pain I have experienced in my life is nothing compared to what some of these youngsters have had, and in some cases still have to, endure.

Hassan was born healthy. But his mother didn't want him, so she systematically beat him to within an inch of his life. He now has water on the brain, is blind and is a mess of twisted bones. He receives twenty-four-hour constant loving care at the centre. Then there was Baby A. She was born to a mum with AIDS. There is a high probability that she also has the virus. As I held her in my arms, I couldn't help thinking about my own daughters Misha and Jodie, and how different their births had been. In Baby A's deep brown African eyes, I saw the hope for the future. I prayed that she does not carry this hideous disease. But in my heart I feared the worst.

The witchdoctors of Uganda propagate the false notion that if a man has AIDS, he can rid himself of the disease by sleeping with a virgin. So that's what sometimes happens – because of ignorance, fear and lack of education. We recently received an email from Kathleen, a friend of ours working with AIDS patients on the Sesse islands. She was comforting a five-year-old girl who had been raped by a man carrying the AIDS virus.

Where is God in all of this? It's a good question. But I believe he is in the hearts of all the aid workers, missionaries and other souls who are prepared to give up all they have for the sake of those who have nothing.

We went to try and help and yet – we were the ones who came away blessed. We went to serve and we came away served.

While we were there, we asked people to tell their story. One young lady in her mid-twenties stood up and, with her best friend by her side to support her physically, emotionally and spiritually, she gave her testimony. Her father had been killed in the war. She later found out that it was her uncle who had killed him, and many others. After the war it was known in the local community that he had perpetrated these acts. Being frightened, he went to the witchdoctor. The witchdoctor told him that he must sacrifice the children, one on each day. There were four in all. On day one, her brother was killed, on day two her sister, on day three another sibling. She should have been sacrificed on day four. But she lay in bed, seriously ill with a high fever. Satisfied that she too would die, her uncle left her. But by God's grace she recovered. The uncle then went on to rape her mother, impregnating her and a half-sister was born.

The uncle lives in a village not far from New Hope. The young woman said she was going to meet him and forgive him in Jesus' name, and then ask him to be her father. She was also going to embrace her half-sister and look after her.

Surely only God can move hearts to this extent.

I wept. I wept for the young woman and the pain she had endured. I wept tears of joy to see the divine transformation in her life.

From hate to love.

If anything can illustrate the power of the Christian message then what I saw and heard that day has to define it.

The Kasana Children's Centre at New Hope Uganda has the fragrance of Jesus in the air. It is a sanctified Garden of Eden, where an open heaven reigns. Jesus is the tangible hope on this dusty landscape.

The contrast between my world and this one could not have been starker. Imagine travelling First Class to Los Angeles, being picked up in a limo and meeting some of the most powerful people in the entertainment world. Then imagine travelling to Uganda, arriving in a mosquito-ridden arrivals hall, walking into a wall of heat, and then bouncing around in a bumpy ride over potholed roads, to meet some of the most powerless people on the planet.

Yet Uganda was the place that stole my heart. It remains, as Churchill described it, 'the pearl of Africa', at times verdant and lush, at other times punishing and unforgiving. Uganda is tainted by all that it has seen. Yet it is a survivor.

It makes everything I've worked hard to achieve over thirty years almost seem worthless. But even I experienced hope there.

One of the great joys of the trip was to write a song with Jonnes Bakimi (one of the founding fathers of New Hope along with Jay Dangers) and the children of Kasana in Ugandan called 'Tata walli', which means 'the Father is here'. Every day I'd learn a new line. By the end of the week we had a new song written between us all.

Yes, I've had the privilege of working with million-selling artists and having numerous hit records over thirty years. But the biggest joy I've ever received is to hear the children of Kasana sing that song while they were playing football.

Now that has to be my greatest hit.

ON THE ROAD

AFTER THE FIRE: 1977

May

6	John Peel Club, Gosport
7	Dingwalls, Camden Lock, London
14	Kesteven College, Grantham
16	The Hayworth Club, Abertillery Rose
17	Woods Club, Plymouth (where if you stamped too hard on the stage the power would go off and/or on!)
21	The Albemarle Club, Romford
27	City College, Norwich
30	The Hermit Club, Brentford

June

	The Lodestar, Blackburn
	The Penny Farthing, Ulverston
	The Toll Bar Inn, Egremont
5	Border Terrier Club, Carlisle
6	Tiffany's, Edinburgh (supporting Cado Belle)
7	The Twisted Wheel, Carlisle
9	Princeville Working Men's Club, Bradford
12	Wormwood Scrubs Prison, London
13	The Lord Nelson, London
14	Top Rank, Cardiff
15	The Viaduct, Bath
16	The Dutch House, Mottingham
18	Blue Bell Railway, Haywards Heath

19	The Lakeland Lounge, Accrington
20	The Lion Hotel, Warrington
21	The Blue Bell, Chesterfield
23	The Marquee, London
24	The Pavilion, Matlock
25	The Rock Garden, Middlesbrough
29	Wye College, Ashford

Here's the rest of my diary for 1977:

July

4–5	ATF play on Ishmael album *It's Amazing What Praising Can Do*
10	Open Air Gig Tower Hamlets Park, London
11	The Nag's Head, High Wycombe
18	Half Moon Theatre, London
23	Andy and Judy's Wedding

August

14	The City Tavern, Chelmsford
19	Haddon Hall Hotel, Leeds
20	Priory Hotel, Scunthorpe
24	The Stapleton Tavern, Stroud Green, London
27	The Greenbelt Festival

September

1	The Old Granary, Bristol
10	Christchurch Hall, Chatham
24	Central Hall, Lytham St Annes

November

3	The Drill Hall, Lincoln
4	City College, Norwich
6	St George's Church, Harold Hill
7–11	ICC Studios, Eastbourne start recording *Signs of Change*
14–18	ICC Studios, Eastbourne
21–25	ICC Studios, Eastbourne
27	Lea Abbey Students Club, London

28–29   ATF play on Andy McCarroll album, ICC Studios,
        Eastbourne
30   November/1st December – mixing album

December
2   The Highcliffe, Margate
3   New Addington
4   St George's Church, Harold Hill
5   The Hermit Club, Brentwood
6–7   Mixing album
9   Norwich: My Last Gig

At some point I rejoined the band for a one-off gig at
Strathclyde University in Glasgow, but cannot recall the
date.

FISH CO: 1978

July
7   Aylesbury
8   Aller Farm, Dawlish
14   Hoddesdon
22   Egham Festival
29   Upstream Theatre, London

August
7–8   Gorinchen, Holland
9–11   Harderwijk, Holland
12   Drachten, Holland
13   Zwolle, Holland
14   A Barge, Amsterdam, Holland (my twenty-first
        birthday)
15   Town Square & Dockside, Amsterdam, Holland
18   Boddy's Music Inn, Amsterdam, Holland
19   Kamperland Festival, Kamperland, Holland
21   TBC, Velbert, Germany
23   Old Daddy's Club, Duisberg, W. Germany
25–28   Greenbelt Festival, Odell, Bedfordshire

September
14–15   Crocker's, Bristol
27   College, Derby, Lonsdale
29   Dartington College of Art
30   Brunel Tech, Bristol

October
2   North Staffs Polytechnic
4   Southampton University
5   Hexagon Theatre, Reading (supporting Marshall Hain)
7   Plymouth Polytechnic (Bram Tchaikovsky and Crawler)
8   Loughborough Polytechnic
11   St Mary's College, Twickenham
14   The Salt Cellar, Bristol
31   Worcester College(?), Oxford

November
3   YMCA, Cambridge
4   Church Hall, St Helens
10   Worcester Polytechnic
17   Frinton-on-Sea
22   Pontypridd Polytechnic
27   Colston Hall, Bristol with Roy Castle
28   Motherwell Civic Centre with Parchment
29   Leeds University with Parchment

December
2   Free Trade Hall, Manchester with Parchment

WRITZ: 1978

UK
November
7   Sheffield Polytechnic (supporting Thompson Twins)
25   Haywards Heath

December
1   Exeter University (with Simple Minds and Renaissance)

1979

January

4–5	Crocker's Club, Bristol
10	Stowaway Club, Newport, Wales
12	Barbarella's, Birmingham
14	Band On The Wall, Manchester

February

2	Country Club, Kirklevington
8	Brunel Rooms, Swindon
9	Bath College of Art
10	Bishop Otter College, Chichester
14	Guildford Agricultural College
21	Bogart's, Birmingham
22	Pontypridd Polytechnic, Wales
23	Exeter University (with The Darts)
24	Swansea University
27	Trent Polytechnic, Middlesex

March

1	RAF, Yeovil
2	Reading University
3	Thamesview School, Gravesend
7	St Mary's College, Twickenham
10	College of St Mark & St John, Plymouth
16	St Luke's College, Exeter
22	HMS Culdrose, Helston, Cornwall
29	HMS Drake, Plymouth

April

20	Assembly Hall, Framlington
27	Barbarella's, Birmingham

May

1	Brunel Rooms, Swindon
4	Middlesex Polytechnic, London
5	The Granary, Bristol

HOLLAND

11	Tin Pan Alley, Emmen
12	Bijenkorf, Enschede
13	Gigant, Apeldoorn
15	Downtown, Den Haag
16	Vilenstede, Amstelveen
18	O'16 Club, Voorburg
22–23	Longenburg Swimming Pool, Velbert (West Germany!)
24	Boelwerk, Sneek
25	Doornroosje, Nijmegen
26	Eland, Delft
27	Boddy's Music Inn, Amsterdam
31	AOR Student Centre, Eindhoven

June

1	De Meule, Heesch
2	Paard van Troje, Den Haag

UK

7	Rock Garden, London
8	Bishop Otter College, Chichester (with Voyager)
9	Dartford Teacher Training College
12	Trent Polytechnic, Nottingham
14	Routes Club, Exeter
15	The Pavilion, Exmouth
16	College of St Mark & St John, Plymouth
23	Reading College
26	Golden Lion, Fulham, London
27	400 Club, Torquay

July

4	Music Machine, London
13	Dingwalls, London
15	The Nashville, London
20	The Limit, Sheffield
27	Music Machine, London (with The Vapors)
28	The Granary, Bristol
29	Memorial Hall, Newbridge
31	Brunel Rooms, Swindon

August

1	Bogart's, Birmingham
4	Leisure Centre, Stroud
11	JB's, Dudley
12	Fforde Greene, Leeds
15	The Stowaway, Newport, Wales
16	The Troubadour, Port Talbot, Wales
17	Routes Club, Exeter
18	Porterhouse, Retford
23	Video – BBC Bristol
24	Sandpiper, Nottingham
25	Bircotes Leisure Centre, Retford
31	The Village, Newport, Shropshire

September

1	Music Machine, London
2	Golden Lion, Fulham, London
18	The Nashville, London
20	Music Hall, Shrewsbury
21	New College, Durham
28	Preston Polytechnic
29	St Katherine's College, Liverpool
30	Fforde Greene, Leeds

October

1	Romeo & Juliet's, Doncaster
2	Brunel Rooms, Swindon
3	Sheffield Polytechnic
5	Seale Hayne College, Newton Abbot
7	Fulham Greyhound, London
10	St Mary's College, Twickenham
11	Music Machine, London
12	Warwick University
13	Reading University
14	Memorial Hall, Newbridge
16	Bindles, Barry
19	Oxford Polytechnic
20	Portsmouth Polytechnic
25	Sheffield University

26   COLCHE, Liverpool
27   Southampton University
31   Trinity College, Carmarthen

November
1   Middlesbrough Town Hall

HOLLAND
11   Vera Club, Groningen
14   Vilenstede, Amstelveen
15   Paard van Troje, Den Haag
16   Gigant, Apeldoorn
17   De Meule, Heesch
18   De Melkweg, Amsterdam

FRANCE
19   Theatre Le Palace, Paris
20   La Colline, St Symphoren D'Ozon, Lyon
22   La Melodie, Brest

December
IRELAND
1   Belfield University, Dublin,

UK
6   The Marquee, London
7   City of London Polytechnic
10   Exeter University (with Renaissance and Simple
      Minds)
12   Café Royale, London
13   Taunton Youth Centre
14   North Staffordshire Polytechnic, Stafford
15   Music Machine, London

DISCOGRAPHY

MUSICIAN/SONGWRITER/PRODUCER/ EXEC. PRODUCER

After the Fire: *Signs of Change* album – Bass/Violin/Vocals
Ishmael: *Amazing* album – Bass
Andy McCarroll: *Epitaph for a Rebel* album – Bass
Iva Twydell: *Waiting for the Son* album – Backing Vocals/Violin
Writz: 'Nightnurse' single – Bass
Writz: album – Bass
Mark Williamson: 'Junior' from the album *Get the Drift* – Songwriter/Bass
Nick Battle: 'Big Boys Don't Cry' from the album *Curious Collection*
Iva Twydell: 'Final Fuse' and 'Get it Right' from the album *Duel* – Producer/Writer
Cliff Richard: 'Take Me to the Leader' – Songwriter: Unreleased
Cliff Richard: 'First Date' from the album *Now You See Me* – Songwriter
Techno Twins: 'Donald and Julie Go Boating' from the album *Technostalgia* – Producer/Songwriter
Sporting Life album – Songwriter/Producer
Cliff Richard: 'Front Page' from the album *Silver* – Songwriter
Jump The Nile: 'Like the Cruel Sea' single – Songwriter
Smalltown Elephants: 'Walking on Ice' single – Songwriter
The Alarm: *Eye of the Hurricane* album – Exec. Producer
Karel Fialka: 'Hey Matthew' single – Exec. Producer
Colin Blunstone: 'Cry an Ocean' single – Exec. Producer
Lypbox: 'My House' single – Exec. Producer

Dennis Greaves & The Truth: *God Gave Rock and Roll to You* album – Exec. Producer.

One Nation: *Strong Enough* album – Exec. Producer

Graystoke: 'Up on the Roof' single – Producer

Graystoke: 'Perfect is the Girl' single – Songwriter/Producer

Generator feat. Gary Numan: 'Are Friends Electric', 'Bring Back the Love' and 'Going Home' – Songwriter/Exec. Producer

Blak Mayl: 'Evri Budi Go' – Exec. Producer

Speed: album – Exec. Producer

Nick Battle: *Songs of Love and Mercy* – Vocal/Guitars/Bass

Nick Battle: *Soaking in the Spirit* album – Guitars/Keyboards/Producer

Fame Academy: 'True Colours' – Bass

Phixx: 'Creepin' – Songwriter

Natasha Bedingfield: 'Don't Pretend' – Songwriter: Unreleased

The Honeyriders: *Letting the Light In* album – Exec. Producer

Michael Ball: 'What Love is For' – Songwriter/ Exec. Producer

Michael Ball: 'When You Tell Me, That You Love Me' – Exec. Producer

Michael Ball: 'This is the Moment' – Exec. Producer

Engelbert Humperdinck: 'Three Words Ain't Enough' – Songwriter/Exec. Producer

Engelbert Humperdinck: *Let There Be Love* album – Exec. Producer

Michael Ball: *Music* album – Exec. Producer

Michael Ball: 'I Am Loved' – Songwriter/Exec. Producer

Russell Watson: 'I Have Nothing' – Exec. Producer

Michael Ball: *One Voice* album – Exec. Producer

Kipper: 'We Come in Peace' – From the album *This is Different* – Songwriter

FILM

Bring Me the Head of Mavis Davis: 'Bring Back the Love' – Songwriter

Some of the artists I've been fortunate enough to plug and promote

Sometimes we were hired for a week, a month and even a year. Normally though it would be for the 'life of the record'.

George Benson & Patti Austin
Black
Jonathan Butler
Capercaillie
Clannad
Deep Purple
Alan Price
David Essex
David Grant
Southside Johnny & The Asbury Jukes
Cliff Richard
Dennis Greaves & The Truth
29 Palms
N.K.O.T.B
Nu Colours
Future Sound Of London
Paul Hardcastle
Arthur Baker & Al Green
Squeeze
John Martyn
Talking Heads
Thunder
Gene Pitney
Kevin Ayers
Take That
Frank Ifield & The Backroom Boys
Ronnie Wood
Courtney Pine
Andy Sheppard
David Hasselhoff

There were many more but I can't remember them all . . .

To contact Nick please email:

NICK.BATTLE@mac.com

Or write to:
PO Box 375
Chorleywood
Herts
WD3 5ZZ

For further information on New Hope Uganda and how you
can help the orphans, please contact:
www.newhopeuganda.org

For further information and how you can help the fight
against cancer please contact:
www.abreast.org.uk
www.cancerbackup.org.uk
www.MarieCurie.org.uk

THANK YOU

Nick Battle

NEW ALBUM FROM NICK

LET GO AND LET GOD

£9.99

Available November 2007 from

Authentic Media